VEERNI

VEERNI

*A journey of female
enlightenment and empowerment*

JACQUELINE DE CHOLLET

UNICORN

First published by Unicorn
an imprint of Unicorn Publishing Group, 2024
Charleston Studio
Meadow Business Centre
Lewes BN8 5RW

www.unicornpublishing.org

ISBN 978-1-916846-16-6

Cover design by Unicorn
Typeset by Vivian Head

Printed in Malta by Gutenberg Press

CONTENTS

INTRODUCTION
A Shawl in Rajasthan

Only the impossible is worth doing.
Akong Rinpoche

For me India has always been somewhere else, close, sometimes incomprehensible, often captivating. I've loved India, I've loved the villages that live outside the world, at their own pace, I've loved the women who are so brave, so joyful, whose language I couldn't speak, yet who welcomed me and shared their laughter and their meals with me. I remember with feeling the dances and songs that united us without our understanding one another, strangers to one another, but sisters in an affinity that sprang from beyond time and place. I loved this world, and yet what was I doing to make it better, to help the women of this country, the poorest of the poor?

Then one day in 1992 I found myself with two friends in a dusty village in Rajasthan, a forgotten corner of the world close to the Pakistani border. How did I get there? My memory doesn't show me arriving near this unknown woman, but I was on her doorstep... She was still young, but her body was tired, worn, her gesture heavy, a baby in her arms and other children running around. She was weaving a colourful shawl and I thought it would be a good idea to help her out a little by buying this square of fabric into which she had poured her energy, her taste, her traditions... I put a few rupees on the table, the asking price. Did the coins jingle? No doubt. In any case, at that moment the husband jumped up and, without a word, under the woman's empty and disillusioned gaze, he took the coins and disappeared as silently as he had come. This woman had managed to make something, then sell it, and by the time she had done so the money had been taken from her. She had no way of defending herself.

Wasn't I, too, that silent woman? Of course, the life of the woman in Rajasthan and mine seemed to have nothing in common. And yet in my Swiss childhood in Fribourg I also experienced a kind of confinement and submission. In that rigorously Catholic town women of my generation could hope for nothing more than to become attentive mothers and exemplary housewives. No one cared to listen to us, no one thought of letting us live out our hopes. University was out of the question; at a pinch, perhaps, we could apply for secretarial school, which would be quite sufficient for girls. There too no one would defend us.

This woman in Rajasthan had no rights. Who cared about her? Who spoke up for her? Who defended her? That's how I wanted to act. And my life was changed.

Those famous women's rights enshrined in United Nations resolutions mean nothing if they don't apply to the woman I'd just met. As Eleanor Roosevelt said, 'Where do human rights begin? In small places, close to home, so close and so small that they cannot be seen on any maps of the world.' These are the places where every woman seeks equal justice, equal opportunity, equal dignity.

I still had to give the project a name. In Indian eyes I was a British aristocrat, and later, when I arrived in Jodhpur for the inaugural trip of the health team, I was surprised to find that on the medical van the following words had been painted in large letters: 'Lady Weir Project'. By then I was divorced from Viscount Weir, but it remained my name. Worse still, this pretentious denomination sent out a bad message. Didn't these terms suggest a little too much of the British Raj, the colonial regime formerly established in India? An effort had been made to promote the project under this name. We had to move away from it. My Indian friend Maja Daruwalla came up with the solution: it would be 'Veerni'. *Veer* means 'hero' in Hindi, and *ni* means 'woman'. So 'Veerni' means 'female hero' – heroine. It couldn't be better!

For almost thirty years the Veerni Project's mission has been to provide women in India's poorest regions with the support they need to make their daily lives a little easier. It took patience, skill and diplomacy to confront the fathers in the villages, fathers who were furious, sure of their rights, convinced that we had come to poach their daughters.

We fought against malnutrition, and finally we took care of women's health and brought some education to the villages. Gentle programmes to tame the men and help the women. Then, slowly, we were allowed to take young girls to Jodhpur, the big city, to open the doors to the best schools.

The problem of girls' malnutrition extends to female infanticide. I've known several dramatic cases: if the mothers gave birth to a girl, they didn't feed her and left her to die. We were able to remedy this to some extent, although in the 1990s this atrocious practice was carefully hidden. But the Veerni Project saved several little girls, who survived and grew up! One of them was called Badami. She lived in a very poor village called Uchiyarda. Her mother already had a daughter, and the grandmother absolutely wanted a boy! As a result, they didn't feed her. In addition, her father had burned her neck with a red-hot iron, to chase away demons. We had baby porridge given by an English organisation, and we gave it to the mother with instructions on how to feed her daughter. We watched the little one every week... and she survived! She became one of my favourites among the young women we rescued in the villages; I brought her dresses from Provence, of which she was very proud.

Her grandmother always told me to take her to 'Am'rica'.

A little later, a new kind of violence against women began to spread. With advances in ultrasound technology, women were sometimes forced to have abortions if they were expecting a girl. Sex selection!

That said, in the last thirty years or so there has been significant progress. Electricity has arrived in the villages, and above all they all benefit from Internet connections that would make many a French village jealous! Links in India work remarkably well. They have gone from medieval times to the linked-up world, and know all about WhatsApp groups and other applications. A revolution that could well change the face of India and the future of Indian women.

Even mental attitudes are changing. In the past, fathers looked at us with suspicion and found it hard to entrust their daughters to us to take them to school. Today, faced with the reality of male violence and the horror of early marriages, they come to us with a request: 'You absolutely must educate our daughters.'

With the help and support of so many people of good will we have set up a training programme for young girls: thanks to the Veerni Project, they are escaping social damnation, learning a trade, and earning a living. The man is no longer the sole provider of funds: the woman becomes independent! More than two hundred girls have been able to escape their condition, become computer specialists or nurses, shopkeepers or civil servants… I know all this is just a drop in the ocean, but even a tiny drop spreads into the sea, perhaps to transform it. Isn't the ocean made up of drops?

I
The Sources of my Action

A woman is the full circle.
Within her is the power to create,
nurture and transform.

Diane Mariechild

Fribourg is a contradictory city, chilly and bold, devout and sovereign. Fribourg shuts itself in, curls itself up and lets itself sink into the chasm that opens to the Sarine. The city seems to fall towards the river, only to rise again and reach the bridge above it.

In the old days when you were from Fribourg, a passionate and devout Catholic, the alliance of families posed a delicate problem: to whom was one going to affiance the young lady of the house or the young man returning from military service? Proudly French-speaking, like half the population of Fribourg, one wasn't going to look for the ideal spouse in German-speaking Switzerland. Nor was one going to turn to French-speaking Switzerland, a land of Protestants, and even less to the Valais, which was undoubtedly Catholic, but populated by rough peasants! So, one had to look to Italy or France. Fribourg was an inland town, but it cultivated a taste for the outside world. For example, my paternal grandmother came from a Catholic family of twelve children from Lyons. Fribourg, both French-speaking and Catholic, is the most European city in Switzerland.

When I think of my childhood, it is the taste of Fribourg that comes to my lips, it is Fribourg that I feel, its cobbled streets that climb towards an improbable elsewhere, the fresh air you breathe when spring covers the hillsides with green, its cathedral of St Nicolas of which the tower dominates the city – my memories cling to Fribourg, and yet I was born in Paris. It was just before the war.

The story of my parents, who lived between Boston, New York, Paris and Fribourg, via Saint-Jean-de-Luz and Lyons, is a strange patchwork of love, adventure and espionage that has always fascinated me. My father, Louis de Chollet, had studied at the École des Hautes Études Commerciales in Paris, then left for the United States to try and make his fortune, because he was as poor as Job. His own father, who had emigrated to Argentina, had ruined himself in unsuccessful ventures.

So, my father arrived in New York in 1928, a poor penniless immigrant that I imagine washing cars to try to survive. Within a few years business was looking up for him; he was working in finance on Wall Street, and that is no doubt when he came upon art and the Impressionists. He was living with the Durand-Ruels, who let a room to him in the attic of their luxurious New York residence. The Durand-Ruel galleries in France, Great Britain and the United States were among the first to understand the pictorial revolution brought about by Monet, Pissarro, Sisley, Renoir and others – great names that now seem to belong to art history, but who was interested in them in the 1930s? Just a few Swiss and a handful of Americans. That is why the great private collections of Impressionist paintings are mostly to be found across the Atlantic or in Winterthur! In the world of the Durand-Ruels, no doubt with their advice, my father discovered and came to love the Impressionists and was able to put together a fine collection, of which some paintings ended up in great museums.

Back to pre-war New York, when my father met my mother, a young woman as beautiful as she was enterprising and independent, a Boston Protestant whose ancestors were said to have landed from the famous *Mayflower* in 1620. She had just been divorced and already had two children – a girl and a boy – but that did not prevent her from leading a bohemian life in the Big Apple, all the more carefree because she had acquired a handsome sum of money at the time of her separation.

Louis and Frances – my parents – married in 1937, but they weren't to stay in America very long. Soon, at the request of his boss, the stockbroker Stanley Halle, my father established an 'information office' in Paris to help persecuted Jews transfer their money to the United States. My parents moved into a beautiful apartment on the Quai d'Orsay, and I was born shortly afterwards.

In May 1940 my parents and I took a trip to New York. We returned to Europe on the worst possible date, 23 May, on the *Conte de Savoya*, a luxury Italian liner for which it was the last crossing before the global conflagration.

We did not leave occupied Paris until the end of May, when I was two years old and my mother was six months pregnant. Memories are of course hazy, but I think my parents lived as if the war did not exist. They did not really believe in the war, although it had already broken out. My father was Swiss and American, my mother American. Coming from two neutral countries, how could they be affected by a conflict that did not concern them? Not yet.

That summer they rented a house in Saint-Jean-de-Luz. In a letter that my mother wrote in 1994, shortly before her death, she told the circumstances of my sister's birth, of which I knew nothing. In September 1940 my mother left the Basque country and arrived in Paris alone. The American Hospital had been requisitioned by the Germans, so she went to give birth all by herself in a clinic in Boulogne-Billancourt. Then in August 1941 my father was denounced for his activities on behalf of the Jews, and our English nanny was arrested at dawn one morning by the Gestapo and held in an internment camp until the end of the war.

For his part my father, alerted by the Swiss Legation, learned that he must leave as soon as possible. Pierre, his elder brother, was working in the Free Zone for Lait Mont-Blanc powdered milk, and was able to obtain official papers for my father as an employee of that company. To leave the occupied zone, however, the documents had to be stamped by a Gestapo office. My mother's birthplace, Philadelphia, posed a problem for the German officer. 'Where is Philadelphia?' 'In Seine-et-Oise,' my father replied at once. Everything is in order!

We all took the train to Lyons, where my mother moved into a small hotel with my sister. And me, a three-year-old? I stayed with my father. Where did I stay? I don't know. But when my mother saw me again, after two or three days, I didn't feel right, and above all I had a terrible squint!

I was cross-eyed for a very long time. I couldn't see well, I bumped into things, I even fell down a lot, and at school I was cruelly called 'the cross-eyed one'! I have photographs of myself as a child where there is no sign of squinting; then photographs taken in Switzerland in 1941 show a little girl squinting horribly. Dismal!

What could have happened? Why does a child suddenly start squinting? I recently asked my doctor, and he told me that such squinting was certainly the result of a trauma. Yes, but what trauma? Neither my father nor my mother mentioned it. What happened to me in those three days?

My whole childhood was marred by this handicap, which I could not overcome at the time. My sister, who was so pretty, was the favourite; my father called her Sunshine, and she was indeed his sunshine. I was the unloved one, loved by neither my mother nor my father. I carried the handicap for a long time: I underwent a first operation at the age of twelve but it was unsuccessful, and I was not rid of the problem until much later, at twenty-seven, after a second operation carried out in

England by a wonderful surgeon who changed my life.

I confess that I have some trouble understanding what went on in my parents' heads. Why these convolutions in occupied France? Risk-taking? Indifference? Ignorance? In any case, that is how we arrived in Fribourg, my father's stronghold. We settled in Guintzet, the hill above Fribourg, in a magnificent 'maison de maître' that had been the summer residence of my great-grandparents. This beautiful house was in an advanced state of disrepair when we arrived, but like a good enterprising American my mother had it all redone, organising the renovation of the building from cellar to attic.

This house, like Fribourg as a whole, became a melting pot of resistance and reflection during the war and in the years that followed. We met the American Allen Dulles of the OSS, refugees from all over Europe, British agents, Italian families including the Agnelli, the head of the Federal Police, and a few Germans... For some German families, openly anti-Nazi, had found a land of freedom and expression on the banks of the Sarine, as well as universities where young people disturbed by the conflict could study in peace.

We were also still receiving children from France who had been driven out of their country by the Occupation, little refugees who had passed through a reception camp in Switzerland but then had to be taken in by a volunteer family. So it was that I, the unloved and unhappy little girl, found my own sunshine. It was Jeanine, a little girl five years older than me, a refugee from Belfort where her Polish parents lived. Lonely as I was, in her I found a sister in distress, an ally in sorrow, and I think she saved my life by preventing me from sinking completely into depression.

Jeanine should then have left us and gone home. But she didn't leave, because I wouldn't let her! When she was due to leave Fribourg I cried a lot, a scene so heartbreaking that my mother took fright: I was five years old, and I said that if Jeanine left, I'd go with her! Jeanine did not leave.

Returning temporarily to Paris in 1945, my mother wanted her American car back, a grey Packard convertible that she had hidden in a garage in Neuilly. She opened the bonnet, fixed the engine, and drove it, all by herself, to Fribourg!

In the following year my parents wanted to return to their Paris apartment, which had been requisitioned by the Germans. That meant a family journey in the car and a three-hour stop at customs, where French officials practically dismantled the car to check for any black market!

When we arrived at our apartment on the Quai d'Orsay, we were devastated! The Louis-Philippe furniture was in pieces, the fireplaces ripped out, and the living room ransacked. My sister and I were stunned and shocked; for us, it was the image of the war we had escaped.

In 1948 family life in Fribourg was profoundly disrupted by my parents' separation: my sister, Jeanine and I went to live with my mother in Paris, and we were placed in the Couvent des Oiseaux school on the rue de Ponthieu. On the way there we were forbidden to use the Arcades du Lido, as we might have discovered indecent photos there. So we took the rue Lancaster and its charming prostitutes!

Shortly afterwards, my mother married an American general, Foster Tate, hero of the Italian campaign, military attaché in Paris, decorated by General de Gaulle. Having decided to return to the United States, she relinquished custody of her children and sent us back to our father in Fribourg. I didn't see my mother again for several years.

Fortunately, however, she took Jeanine with her, because I don't think there was any future for the daughter of a Polish immigrant in Fribourg at that time. The United States gave my dear Jeanine a chance that she seized: she got married, had two children… I've always kept in touch with her, whom I've never stopped thinking of as my sister.

Jeanine was able to make a life for herself in the United States because over there the question is not 'Who are you?' but 'What are you doing?' Nobody cares about the past, about family, about ancestors… People come from all over the US – they're born in one state, they go to live in another, they go to university here, they go to work somewhere else. In Europe, chatter, backbiting and gossip readily classify people according to family and origin. In the United States that nonsense is irrelevant because everyone is from everywhere.

Today I have American grandchildren: their grandfather was the son of a Cretan villager who landed penniless on Ellis Island, New York's immigrant reception centre. He started out working in a tannery in Pennsylvania and his six children all went on to extraordinary careers: one was a physics professor at Yale University, another an influential Orthodox pope, a third a brilliant financier. That's America. There's great social mobility there, but you have to make the effort to succeed. In the United States if you don't succeed, don't look for responsibility elsewhere: it's your own fault! Europe, on the other hand, is Freudian – nothing is your fault, it's always someone else's! Personally, I have much more sympathy for America, because it opens up all possibilities.

My father was an important figure in Fribourg, and our house on the Guintzet soon resembled an international aviary where artists, politicians and more or less discreet spies crossed paths. My father knew everyone through his professional contacts in America, France and Switzerland. For business, he lived in Paris, on the Avenue George V, where he had a beautiful apartment, because he loved only France, considered himself French, and most of his friends were from France… He was a brilliant man, an international banker who worked with Wall Street establishments, with the Union de Banques Suisses, with the Rothschild Bank... He had that American mentality of daring and originality, always proposing an innovative vision, a different organisation. But he was a complicated, anxious character, who'd had a difficult childhood and never found peace in life.

After my mother's departure and their divorce, my father married Roselyne Radziwill née de Monleon, who was half French and half from Fribourg. Her father, Count Guy de Monléon, was a heroic figure of the First World War dying in August 1914.

Growing up in Fribourg, a very catholic town could be somewhat suffocating. Constraints, it's true, but life was interesting and many years later, around 1995, I met Balthus again in London at the home of the Swiss ambassador to the UK. 'But she's not squinting anymore!' he cried. He remembered.

How could I not also mention the German painter Dietz Edzard? He had painted my portrait as a child, then a new one for my eighteenth birthday. It was a way of thanking my father, who had helped him during the war to leave Paris and his studio on the rue des Saints-Pères to take refuge in New York. It was in the studio there that I had posed after the Liberation.

In Fribourg I was educated at La Chassotte, an international boarding school for girls run by the Fidèles Compagnes de Jésus, a congregation that was for a time an offshoot of the Jesuits and also flourished in Great Britain.

I remember having to pay special reverence to an Italian saint named Stromboli, or something similar. I didn't understand this adoration for a woman who had never been a mother. Why do we celebrate a virgin when we're supposed to be on Earth to bear children? A question the nuns should never have been asked!

At La Chassotte I was suffocating from an air so infected with rigorism and bigotry. Religion was certainly intense, but there was a new contradiction: everything was allowed in Fribourg during the carnival in February. For three days the Church turned a blind eye to all excesses, mockery and quips. Sometimes I think that Fribourg, with all its antagonisms, is perhaps the most interesting city in Switzerland, the most original without doubt, and I sometimes have the impression that it crystallises the entire history of the confederation... We must never forget that we were occupied by the Habsburgs and that we fought against the French, notably at the Battle of Morat in 1476. Independence was no empty word!

Yet Swiss mercenaries were famous throughout the armies of Europe: some of my Chollet ancestors, originally from Gruyère, fought in Louis XVI's troops, while others fought for Spain. Poor people from a poor country, they enlisted in the cohorts that were willing to take them on, fighting for the foreigner, fighting to survive, but never forgetting their country. Isn't it said that Swiss mercenaries deserted en masse when they heard 'le Ranz des Vaches', the song of the Fribourg shepherds? 'Les armaillis des Colombettes de bon matin se sont levés...' (The herdsmen of the Colombettes rose early in the morning). It was forbidden to play this tune in the armies of the King of France, and death to anyone who muttered this hymn of cow herding!

Later, my great-great-uncle brought our family name into the realm of philanthropy: this Louis de Chollet – whose first name my father bore – set up a foundation around 1890 to help young Fribourgeois from disadvantaged families pursue long studies. This 'Caisse des scholarques' still exists today, and as a reminder my grandfather's bust stands in the town hall and a street near the university bears his name.

My paternal grandmother's brother was Adolphe Messimy, a name that has gone down in French history, a Dreyfusard general, Minister of War just before 1914, an astonishing character whom my father knew well and adored. This politician general had shown immense courage in his support for Captain Alfred

Dreyfus, the Jewish officer falsely accused of espionage. Messimy had been expelled from the army, and even his own parents had rejected him as anti-Catholic and unpatriotic! Rehabilitated, the general joined the Caillaux government in 1911, then fought valiantly on the front in the First World War.

As for me, although my schooling was initially tinged with intransigent religious rigidity, I was eventually to discover the astonishing contrasts of Fribourg: when the time came for me to prepare for my first baccalaureate, I changed schools. I was enrolled in a Dominican convent just outside Fribourg, in Pensier. My life changed radically! I was still in a strictly religious establishment, but what happiness to discover an observance lived with joy, relaxation and a smile... I learned to loosen the overpowering straitjacket of religion and bite into life with happiness.

I remember with emotion and gratitude Mother Ancilla, a cheerful Dominican with whom we skied down the snowy slopes of the Moléson. It must be said that there were only three of us. Obviously, in the canton of Fribourg, very few girls were preparing for the French *bac*. But I was there at the behest of my father, who had studied at the École des Hautes Études Commerciales in Paris and was determined that I too should follow a French curriculum.

Our Dominican school in Pensier was a boarding school, but this time my parents allowed me to be a bit of an airhead and go home in the evenings. I was the only day student, and every day I took the train to cover the few kilometres between Fribourg and our school. Adolescence is the age of great attachments, and it was here that I met Dominique Claudel, the granddaughter of the writer Paul Claudel, a friend for many years.

It has to be said that teaching in Fribourg in the post-war years benefitted from the presence of teachers of a rare elevation of spirit. My literature teacher was Pierre-Henri Simon, a future member of the Académie française, who in 1957 published a pamphlet against the war in Algeria entitled *Contre la torture* (Against Torture), which earned him strong enmities in France. There was also Father Joseph-Maria Bochenski, a world-renowned Polish clergyman, philosopher and Sovietologist, author of works against Marxism that are still a reference today.

In the end I took the written part of my first baccalaureate in Thonon and the oral part in Grenoble. As Switzerland was so misogynistic, you couldn't find a school in French-speaking Switzerland for girls who wanted to take the second *bac*. That level was reserved for boys! I had a choice: Paris, where my father had returned to live, or Madrid, where he had some connections. I chose Madrid without hesitation, because it offered the promise of a new life.

There was an excellent French lycée in Madrid, but it was run by Communists obsessed with the class struggle! The philosophy teacher was brilliant, and adored Kierkegaard, so we only studied him... and Marx, of course. By the end of the year, we were all Marxists!

The deputy director was a certain Monsieur Julien, and as I had a particle in my name, which annoyed him, he took extreme care to call me 'Chollet', for short! There was a pupil in the class called Duroux, and he thought it was very clever to call him 'Roux'! 'But, Monsieur, my name is Duroux in a nutshell,' the young man protested. 'Shut up!'

Despite his proudly plebeian stance, the deputy director couldn't play on the non-existent particle of the pupil Simeon – who had been, as a child, the last king of Bulgaria! I don't remember the young boy being taunted by his teachers, but I imagine that a deposed sovereign must have satisfied and reassured the revolutionary spirit of our teachers.

After I graduated my father put me to work in a business of which he was president, l'Office du livre de Fribourg, a Swiss distribution company for French and German publishing houses.

At the time the company was run by Jean Hirschen, a great art book publisher, and for two years I contributed in my own way to the sumptuous works he published, including a fascinating study of the arts of China written by Daisy Lion-Goldschmidt, a project manager at the Musée Guimet in Paris. Then I joined an American company and went to live with my mother in the States. I never came back to live in Fribourg. I couldn't take it anymore, and I lived in terror, fearing more than anything that my father, habit, social pressure and tradition would combine to push me into marriage! A beautiful wedding, of course, complete with cathedral, white dress and wreath of orange blossom. There was no shortage of candidates! A nightmare for me. I saw myself locked up for life somewhere in Switzerland, imagining myself a prisoner in a despairing Jura countryside...

I had to get away, take flight, and I left for a weekend in Southampton, near New York. There, to my great surprise, I was offered a job. A company was looking for a French-speaking secretary, and I immediately accepted. And so, in the days that followed, happy and free, I moved into offices in the most beautiful building on Park Avenue. My life was changing, Switzerland was slipping away. The shifty, unloved Fribourg girl had found her place.

Of course, moving away from the landscapes of my childhood in no way implied a break with my father. I always remained very close to him, despite his difficult character, his anxieties and his mood swings. It seems to me that he lived in a state of permanent stress and nervousness. Was this constant anguish the cause of the malignant tumor that finally took his life in 1972, when he was only sixty-seven years old?

My life in America brought me back to my mother, who was living with her husband, a general, near Washington, in Maryland, a region that was home to many senior officers and former spies who had fought in the war. Decades after the conflict, the area was still teeming with more or less retired secret agents and highly decorated servicemen, all happy to reminisce about their past exploits. It was an interesting enough world for Allen Dulles, then Director of the CIA, to come and sniff the air in my mother's home on a regular basis.

A strange woman, very strong-willed, married three times, my mother was never a mother. She never asked me a single question about my life, my ambitions, my hopes. She rarely phoned me. Once, much later, I organised a musical gala at Buckingham Palace in London for Prince Charles (the future King Charles III), who sent me a lovely letter to thank me. I sent this noble missive to my mother. That letter earned me a phone call! She, who had lived in England, was very impressed by this page from the palace. It took the intervention of the British royal family to earn a phone call from my mother!

If she wasn't a mother to her children, she wasn't a grandmother to her grandchildren either. On the other hand, in the mysteries of life, she was very close to her great-grandchildren. Time had passed, the stakes were gone, what remained was family and the joyful innocence of a new generation.

One day, when she was already in her nineties, she finally asked me a question. Anguish perhaps, approaching the end, she wanted to know: 'What is your life philosophy?'

I replied that the past was an unattainable destination, and that we should always live in the present and look to the future.

'I feel like I'm getting to know you for the first time,' she concluded.

A moving moment that remains intact in my memory.

I was there at her bedside, and I think she was calm and serene. She had an oxygen mask to help her breathe, but she couldn't take it anymore. It was the end. She wanted to be left alone. She ripped the mask off. I didn't give it back. Maybe you have to let people go when life weighs too heavily.

If my troubled family history comes back so insistently to my pen it's because I'm looking for it, because I find in it the origin of my commitments. I think that, in a way, my mother was an authentic feminist. This 'Boston Brahmin' – a term used to describe the aristocracy of New England – led an independent life at a time when women had to blindly obey society's codes. When she came of age her father gave her a car on condition that she learn not only to drive but also to repair the engine – in those days, breakdowns were common. I often saw her with her hands in the grease, proud, original and free. She lived her life the way she wanted to, yet she suffered from a cruel handicap: she had a limp. At the age of eight she had fallen off a wall and been so badly treated that she developed tuberculosis of the bone in her left knee, which stiffened the joint. This infirmity did not prevent her from racing cars, riding horses, skating and walking valiantly until the age of eighty-eight!

In the end, she led her life exactly as she saw fit, and was a role model for me. If I decided to do my bit to change the lot of women, I owe it to her. True, I didn't get to know her well enough, and she didn't raise me, but ultimately, she was the major influence on my life. Because she was indomitable.

II

The Art of the Possible

Each of us is called to change the world,
to work for a culture of life,
a culture forged by love and respect for
the dignity of each human person.
His Holiness Benedict XVI

In 1961 in the United States, I met two British men, Donald and William, each as charming as the other. I married the first, perhaps because I couldn't marry both. Fifteen years later, I married the second.

As soon as I was married, I went to live in Great Britain, a country I knew nothing about. So for several decades my life, my understanding of the world, my evolution in society and the apprehension of my commitments had to take place there. I regretted leaving New York, but Donald Marr, who worked in finance, wanted to return home. My life in London was dedicated to my three children – Alexandra, Sophie and Michael.

It was William, my second husband, by then Viscount Weir and a member of the Bank of England's court, who in 1976 gave me the platform I needed for my commitments and ultimately enabled me to become the woman I am today. With him I travelled all over the world, meeting impressive and influential people, enough to give me self-confidence, to instill in me the ability to develop into a new woman... And again, the marriage eventually fell apart. With these encounters and my struggles, I had changed too much: William wanted a wife devoted to the home, and I wasn't really that anymore. He left with another woman who perhaps better matched the ideal female portrait he had drawn in his mind.

As for me, in 1994 I married for the third time, Robert Towbin, an American who was Jewish. Quite a shock to British society, which couldn't forgive me for giving up my title of viscountess for such a 'mismatch'!

My third husband had been appointed head of an American government investment fund designed to promote the development of capitalism in Russia. We lived intermittently in Moscow for two years, between 1994 and 1996. It was fascinating, but difficult, and I hated this decaying world that had become extremely dangerous. I stayed married for ten years to Robert, a very attractive man, but a ladies' man... I put up with it for a while, and I remained on very good terms with him. Three marriages, three different lives, and this time spent in New York was of enormous benefit to me because my husband knew the whole artistic and cultural scene, an exciting life in which I have continued to flourish.

One of my great advantages, through my family and my contacts, was that I was able to make friends who supported me and helped me enormously in my actions and projects. People who had a clear vision of history. These dear friends are mostly no longer with us. What they had in common was that they had lived through the pre-war, war and post-war periods, which gave them a wealth of experience and a perspective with which better to judge the evolution of the world.

Who can I ask today about the dangers facing our democracies? Things have changed so much since 2000, especially among the British nobility. They have inherited magnificent palaces, but that is not enough: the skill of the English is to recognise talent. All those Jewish immigrants who came from Lithuania, Russia, Hungary, Germany and Poland in the 1930s contributed to English life through philosophy, music and business. What did the English do to assimilate these newcomers? They ennobled them and fully integrated them into English society. For example, the conductor György Stern, born in Budapest, became Sir Georg Solti. These people are absorbed and completely loyal to Great Britain because this country not only gave them a home but offered them a new life by recognising their talent. This was a very clever thing to do, and these people from all over the world became subjects of Her Majesty. But all these extraordinary characters are no longer here today, and we have entered a different world.

But let's go back to my early days in London. I found, on the banks of the Thames, a frozen society where the social ladder was practically blocked. And as someone who evolved there in an aristocratic milieu, I was able to see this immobility of attitudes and a certain social contempt. Things have clearly changed a lot since then.

In terms of the status of women, on the other hand, there is still a long way to go. I remember a visit by Margaret Thatcher to my home in Scotland. It was 1979, she was to become Prime Minister five months later, but she was already leader of the Conservative party. 'Jumped up daughter of a grocer', my husband used to say with disdain. He was wrong: Mrs Thatcher was brilliant, as a scientist and as a politician, and she dominated her audience before she dominated the government. In England and Scotland it was customary at the end of a meal for the men to stay at the table and the women to leave. I said to my husband: 'You're not doing that to Margaret!' He did. What shame, what contempt! The most prominent female politician in the UK found herself with five wives of local administrators talking about their curtains, and I could see her champing at the bit with this humiliation.

I also got to meet Princess Diana. For me, this young woman's life is a Greek tragedy that will disturb the British throne for a long time to come.

I contacted Lady Di to try and persuade her to take the lead in a major worldwide movement for women's causes. 'You're the only one who can fill this role,' I told her. 'Wherever you go, there will be 10,000 or 20,000 people to support you. You will be the champion of women around the world, you will change the condition of women, because people will listen to you.' She didn't want to get involved in this battle. She had exceptional communication skills, of course, but she lacked the ability to turn her celebrity into action. She had left school at fourteen like many Englishwomen of her background. In these aristocratic families, girls did not spend a long time at school and never set foot at university. She could have done so much for teenage girls and women around the world – a missed opportunity that will not reappear anytime soon. In fact, she sometimes found herself completely lost.

The rest is history: she was cut off from the rest of the royal family, living alone in Kensington Palace. What a waste. She could have helped so many people, because finally she spoke well in public. Then she got involved in the fight against AIDS and landmines, necessary and laudable battles, but she could have had greater ambitions, I'm sure.

In 1983 in England, I became involved in social housing through the Southern Housing Group, a London-based association concerned with housing in different parts of the country. The Deputy Governor of the Bank of England had put me on the committee as an organiser, because he was looking for someone capable of developing a new and unexpected vision. I fit the bill: wasn't I both a woman and a foreigner?

It was hard training. I was the only woman, and during meetings some members looked at me sourly and said with contempt: 'There are some people here who have no understanding of finance.' Because, it seems, women don't understand numbers... unlike men, of course!

What's more, by marriage I was then a viscountess, a title that enraged the militant Leftists, who even refused to greet me. The atmosphere became so unbreathable that I went to see the Bank of England official to tell him how difficult it was to work in such a hostile environment, and that I would have to throw in the towel. In response he sent me a magnificent letter in which he not only rejected my resignation but expressed his full support.

The organisation had local committees that included representatives of tenants, notably the West London Committee for certain particularly difficult London neighbourhoods. The tenants' representative was permanently aggressive and unbearable, especially with me. One day I decided to confront him directly: 'If you want me to help you, you're going to have to change your attitude, otherwise my presence among you is pointless, and I'd rather give it all up!'

Incredible as it may seem, his attitude changed completely! He invited me shortly afterwards to open a social centre, and introduced me in terms that moved me greatly: 'She's my friend!'

It was a high point in my militant life, one of the most beautiful things that ever happened to me.

There were a dozen of us on the committee, and I brought in my friend Freddy Fisher, a brilliant journalist of German-Jewish origin, former editor of the *Financial Times*. In all the council flats around London we were called Freddy and Jacqueline, the only members of the committee to be called by our first names – the two foreigners, the German and the Swiss. The others, proudly Left wing, looked down on poverty with contempt, it seemed to me, and the beneficiaries of our actions felt it perfectly.

Fredy was a man of great value. He should obviously have been chairman of the committee, but they did not appoint him. Instead, they appointed me as vice president. I told my friend that I was going to refuse: he should have been appointed! 'Take the job,' he said, 'and I'll always be behind you.' He became my mentor and helped me navigate the complicated waters of administration.

When I left the committee in 1999, after fifteen years of activity, we had gone from 3,000 people housed to 35,000 – quite a success story.

Those years of militancy taught me many things and strengthened my feminist commitment. Who are the poorest housed in the world's slums, from London to Rio to Hong Kong? I've seen it with my own eyes: it's always women. And even more so, minority women. In the Whitechapel Council flats I met women from Bangladesh who were totally isolated, lost, speaking only Sylheti, a Bangladeshi language, cut off from everything because no one could communicate with them, and in addition mothers of large families, sometimes a dozen children.

I realised the extent to which English society was doing nothing to help these women, who were both ignored and unhappy. In the 1960s the British had brought in textile workers, men... They returned home every four years, and every time there was another child. When Margaret Thatcher became Prime Minister she changed all that and allowed family reunification. The Bengali textile workers brought their wives and children with them. But all these people had to be housed. The women arrived from a remote, little-known region where they had their lives and their relationships, and suddenly found themselves stuck and isolated on London's doorstep. There was no need to cross the planet to take an interest in the situation of women: the marginalisation of Bangladeshi women was taking place before our very eyes, at home. In fact, social housing was a vehicle for the status of women.

The experience and influence acquired by this British organisation helped me to develop my activism towards feminism. Yes, it was social issues that led me resolutely to feminism, and

I first wanted to fight in England itself. When you live in a country you have to be part of the life of that country, otherwise you stay on the sidelines and don't understand what is going on. It's urgent to understand, otherwise the social divide will widen.

Social housing in England was poorly built and badly managed, and we had to start from scratch. I made friends with people in Paris who introduced me to the famous Spanish architect Ricardo Bofill. We owe him, for instance, the 'Échelles du Baroque' in Montparnasse, a residential complex that erases the difference between social housing and other housing, creating a new aesthetic where old patterns are swept away.

With the policy of small houses instituted by the former Prince of Wales, social housing is very expensive, so the surface areas granted are tiny. In some of Ricardo Bofill's projects social housing had 30 per cent more square metres for the same number of inhabitants.

We were invited to Barcelona by Bofill. We attended a magnificent presentation of daring and invention, and visited the disused factory he had transformed into apartments on the outskirts of the city. Afterwards we flew to Stuttgart, where we saw German social housing, absolutely dreadful bunkers… The English loved it!

Then I was asked to speak at a conference on social housing. I told them that as architects they should be space analysts. People who have no means of transport are to be brought together. But these people need access to schools, hospitals, football fields and shops. All too often, however, they are relegated to cheap land outside cities.

In Glasgow, Scotland, it is the worst. They have taken the poor out of the slums and put them in council housing outside the city. And to stop these people drinking, or being tempted by alcoholism, there are no bars in the vicinity! The deterioration of the area is complete. A nearby cemetery is very lively: it is the only place where people can meet and find a little human warmth!

Then, the owner of cheap hotels in Scotland opened a pub, the Oasis, and hired buses to take his customers there. I set out to see it. All the furniture was fixed to the floor, ashtrays were dug into the tables, glasses were plastic – all to prevent fights from getting too out of hand. You can't imagine the horror of life around these low-cost housing estates.

In these associations I rubbed shoulders with people who decide what is good for others. No consultation committee whatsoever. The great lesson of these somewhat despairing accounts is that you have to listen. Listen to those you want to help, listen to the people on the ground. Social housing has taught me humility, and humility helps us understand. It's certainly not by dictating to others certain things you think are good that you necessarily do good. It's a lesson I applied when I decided to help young girls in India. We need village consultation committees; we need to listen and ask the people for their opinion.

The strength of our Indian project lies first and foremost in our team, who speak the language of the villages and have spent a lot of time listening, sitting on the ground. If we impose our Western views, we get an idea of what is good for others that is not based on the needs of the locals. In Africa I visited a village in Zambia with my children. An English company had built a magnificent hotel in a very poor village. That company decided to help the village, and announced that they were going to build a school and a hospital. The villagers, with their past experience, said what they needed first was a police station. So the company – a good listener – built the police station, then the school, then the hospital. Without the police to keep an eye on things everything would quickly have been stolen and damaged, the school would have disappeared, and the hospital would not have treated anyone.

In the West we are constantly formulating ideas about the needs of others. As women, too, we judge by our own experience, confusing the potential needs of women over there with the needs of women here. But over there they practise the art of the possible: you have to have the wisdom to know what you can do.

There is a text called *The Serenity Prayer* that is widely used in Alcoholics Anonymous groups, because in public housing alcohol was sometimes a problem. I have visited these centres in America and Hong Kong. No one acts as a judge in these groups, and some are saved! The prayer written by the American theologian Reinhold Niebuhr in the 1930s was a great inspiration to me:

God, grant me the serenity to accept the things I cannot change,
Courage to change the things I can,
And wisdom to know the difference.

It all adds up to a constellation of experiences that form a global picture. Everything is connected. We need to achieve a balance in the way we look at things. Today, it seems to me that NGOs, non-governmental organisations, have lost their ability to listen. They invent programmes and try to impose them.

The art of the possible is not to impose our values but to understand the variety of cultures. We're not here to change their culture, but to provide any help they might need to achieve their goals. As the Indian philosopher Amartya Sen saw it, Indian women are no longer 'passive recipients' of state welfare programmes: they have become active agents of change, agents of social transformation. However, as we can imagine, such upheavals take time and can never be imposed from outside. Once again, the most important part of social transformation for women is education.

In Sierra Leone the UN decided around 2009 that plans had to be drawn up to combat 'gender-based violence'. Funds had been released for this action. I was part of the team. We went to an appalling village. There were about thirty women and fifteen men in a corner. We stood on a platform like important foreign visitors, but with no connection to the population. Someone spoke to say that thanks to the association things had changed, women were respected. Then a woman in the audience stood up and said more or less the same thing.

Did she? I did notice one disturbing thing, though: the ages didn't match! The men were young and the women rather old. I turned to my colleagues and suggested that we split up: some of us would take a group of women, others a group of men. I went and sat down with about twenty women, and they said that they didn't know these men: they had been put together for the day in our honour! In reality, the husbands of these women had been killed during the civil war that began in 1991: they had no money, they had children to feed, they needed to earn a living. At the end I found myself in the middle of these women, and they said to me: 'You are the first person to listen to us.'

These people had been put together for the day, like a show, and the naive UN envoys believed it because they wanted to believe it!

It's like a school in the slums of Bombay, a famous case that some donors supported, that had just been set up for a week, the time it took for generous volunteers to come and admire their work! You can do anything for a week, but you have to stay longer. After a few more days the truth comes out, the fabrication collapses. You must always take time, stay in one place, feel the wind, but people are in such a hurry.

In this way we were visited in India by a European organisation eager to help us with our project. The ladies did us the honour of staying with us for a couple of hours, then went shopping to take home some lovely souvenirs!

Do you know the exemplary and dramatic story of the villages of amputees in Sierra Leone? There, during the war, arms and legs were cut off from the old, the young, children, everyone. In 2002 when the war ended there were cripples everywhere in the streets. Norway and England decided to build three villages for these amputees. They called these villages Norway, London, and Elise, the first name of the Norwegian lady who had conceived the programme. Placed one kilometre from the town of Koidu, and spaced one kilometre apart, these villages are like those for lepers: only handicapped people, cut off from the world, set apart. Houses were built for them but without indoor kitchens, and it rains a lot there. There is a well, but in summer there is no water. They did not build what we did in our villages: gutters with cisterns that fill up with rainwater. These people have married and had children, but most of them can't take their children to school because they can't walk. In short, what have these villages created with the best intentions in the world led to? Even greater difficulties for these wounded beings, now relegated to ill-adapted habitats. The generous Elise knows that a village bears her name, but has she really thought about the consequences of her action?

What should have been done? The first thing, it seems to me, would have been to fit these victims of indiscriminate violence with prostheses, so that they could hope to return to a relatively normal life. Yes, but the fact is that the manufacture of properly adapted prostheses is very expensive, and what is true for adults is even more so for children. For them budgets burst because prostheses have to be replaced almost every year, as the child grows.

So, is it because we don't want to see the problem that we've hidden the disabled away in modern-day leper-houses? An absurd situation! Have the promoters of the project listened to these disabled people?

Why listen when you think you know the absolute truth?

But there is never just one truth: there are many truths, and how do we navigate between them? These questions are rarely asked. I find this sort of dictatorship in international aid extremely disturbing. No one is listening; they stop listening.

III
The Avatars of Feminism

*The battle for women's individual rights
is a long-term battle.*

Eleanor Roosevelt

Am I a feminist? How do I define it? For me today I see feminism as a road to progress, a feminist as a person who understands that we are all human beings and therefore all entitled to equal rights and respect. A feminist knows that the only way to achieve this is actively to educate others. As a result, a feminist will not sit back quietly and allow society to discriminate against anyone due to their sex.

I don't know what this word implies in terms of commitments (often), excesses (sometimes), battles (always). But I do know that women's lives are extremely complicated. Men have a vertical life; we have a horizontal one. We women have to manage a lot of things throughout our lives, including our reproductive system for almost forty years. Men have no equivalent of these multiple obligations. As a result, the demands made on women are often immeasurable.

At least that's what the intimate experiences of my marriages have taught me. As a young girl I was programmed to marry a successful man. But does this ideal figure allow the wife to know who she really is and what she really wants? This supreme husband expresses expectations and ideals that over time seem increasingly difficult to balance with the woman's profound desires. And then, of course, when the woman finally realises who she is and who she wants to be, the attempt at flight no longer suits the man at all! This is clearly what happened with my second marriage: when my husband appreciated that the woman at his side was no longer the woman he had married, he went off with another woman, no doubt more in line with his wishes.

When I look in the rear-view mirror, I see that I married emotionally unstable men three times. They had formed an image of the woman they wanted, and if the woman no longer matched this fantasised vision everything fell apart. I did not feel like playing the role of a trophy wife.

Finally, is seeking one's own path, independently of the idea of appearing as a perfect wife, realising oneself without wanting to correspond to an image constructed by others – is this feminism, or is it simply seeking oneself? Where I'm concerned, if feminism is involved, it serves to build my own personality better. But my activist life has always been marked by women's struggles for education, health and independence.

I've taken part in numerous UN conferences for this feminist cause, or more broadly for human rights. I was in Vienna in 1993 for the World Conference on Human Rights, which resulted in a declaration taking into account 'the various forms of discrimination and violence to which women continue to be exposed throughout the world', and which on this matter concluded with these strong words: 'The fundamental rights of women and girls are an inalienable, integral and inseparable part of universal human rights. The equal and full participation of women in political, civil, economic, social and cultural life, at national, regional and international levels, and the total elimination of all forms of discrimination based on sex are priority aims of the international community.'

I was in Beijing in September 1995 for the Fourth World Conference on Women. The atmosphere was a little surreal, but extraordinary! Just imagine, 40,000 women descended on Beijing to a sort of joyful – and muddy – carnival. Normally it never rains in China at that time of year, but that year it was downpour after downpour! On the sidelines of the conference, the Non-Governmental Organisations Forum was held in a muddy field in Huairou, an hour's drive from Beijing. We had to take buses, but the windows wouldn't shut, and we arrived drenched. The discomfort no doubt didn't displease the Chinese authorities, who were dismayed and perhaps frightened by this abundance of Yin, the feminine energy. In any case, they bored us for three days, multiplying checks and difficulties, and then, having had enough, they gave up and left us alone!

In the exchanges we managed to impose our views despite three states determined to block any progress on sexual and reproductive health rights. Iran and Sudan tried to prevent the slightest progress in these areas, joined by the Vatican, which had dispatched a cohort of brilliant minds skilled in casuistry to maintain the traditional subjugation of women.

Until then there had been no legislation or UN declaration to make a loud and clear assertion of women's rights to health and contraception. Under the determined and courageous leadership of the Conference's Secretary General, Tanzanian Gertrude Mongella, the battle was fierce.

Hillary Clinton launched her famous declaration: 'Women's rights are human rights once and for all!'

Burma's Aung San Suu Ky, winner of the Nobel Peace Prize, strongly condemned all attacks on women's rights.

On the final day, at the moment of the final vote, the representative of Italy, who was speaking on behalf of the European Union, stood up and announced that she could not accept the terms of the resolution. Why was this? Because the Dutch and Swedes had wanted to include lesbian rights in the text. Remember, this was 1995: homosexuality was still a delicate question, and Italy preferred to avoid the subject.

'It's not possible!' the session chair Mervat Tallawy, an Egyptian diplomat, uttered with a choke. 'We've been talking about this for days! Think about it. You have until 8 a.m. tomorrow.'

The African women were calling us crazy, especially the representatives from South Africa, who had come with a multiracial delegation. 'We're fighting not to marry our brothers-in-law with AIDS, and you're talking about lesbian rights!'

The gulf seemed immense; Europe scandalous! In the end a consensus was reached, leading to a more measured resolution on women's rights.

The Beijing experience was fantastic, a fundamental turning point. Our resolutions have had a major influence on future reproductive health programmes, particularly those of UNICEF, the United Nations Children's Fund. Women's health rights are now generally recognised, and this awareness dates back to Beijing. In the conclusion there, 'the Governments participating in the Fourth World Conference on Women' reaffirmed their commitment to a number of points, of which the following was the first:

> The equal rights and inherent human dignity of women and men and other purposes and principles enshrined in the Charter of the United Nations, to the Universal Declaration of Human Rights and other international human rights instruments, in particular the Convention on the Elimination of All Forms of Discrimination against Women and the Convention on the Rights of the Child, as well as the Declaration on the Elimination of Violence against Women and the Declaration on the Right to Development.

The following year, in Istanbul, I was a representative at the second United Nations Conference on Human Settlements. Its aim was to address two major themes of concern to all nations:

– adequate housing for all
– sustainable human settlements in a rapidly urbanising
  world

Here again, in the conclusions, the essential role of women was recognised:

> Women have an important role to play in the attainment of sustainable human settlements. Nevertheless, as a result of a number of factors, including the persistent and increasing burden of poverty on women and discrimination against women, women face particular constraints in obtaining adequate shelter and in fully participating in decision-making related to sustainable human settlements. The empowerment of women and their full and equal participation in political, social and economic life, the improvement of health and the eradication of poverty are essential to achieving sustainable human settlements.

I was able to attend these international conferences as a representative of an American organisation, the International Women's Health Coalition. Based in New York, this dealt with issues relating to rights, health and gender equality, but with a special concern for matters linked to women's health, hence to issues relating to sexuality and reproduction. This non-governmental organisation was founded by an extraordinary Englishwoman, Joan Dunlop, who, 'angered by the rise of the anti-abortion movement in the United States' in 1984, convinced the Rockefeller Foundation to invest in reproductive health. Joan was a magnificent pioneer of women's health and I worked a lot with her. She had a very strong presence and a very British sense of humour. In short, she was a star!

Her organisation had assembled a prestigious board, which

over the years included people as diverse as Bernard Kouchner, founder of Médecins sans Frontières, and Pascoal Mocumbi, Prime Minister of Mozambique. I had the honour of being elected Vice President of this NGO, a position I held until 2000. We organised major fundraising events, and further to defend women's rights around the world I travelled extensively, from Cairo to Beijing. We worked with African women, especially representatives from Nigeria and Cameroon. In the 1990s I accompanied one of them to testify before the United States Congress on the condition of women, in order to convince the members to devote funds to support African women.

In 2019 the International Women's Health Coalition wanted to take a new turn, so they hired an expensive communications agency to promote the organisation, with a new aim: to stress the right of abortion for all. I was asked what I thought of this. Theoretically, of course, how could one not support it? But for those who know the land, the subject is much trickier to handle! I tried to explain that the organisation had to keep global women's health in its sights. For me, putting the spotlight on abortion was a counterproductive decision that could only lead to intense complications. In many countries abortion is practised, whether it is legal or not. Shedding light on this reality risks harming women and further restricting the possibility of abortion. In India, for example, there are four types, depending on the State and the patient's social status: legal and safe, illegal and safe, legal and dangerous, illegal and dangerous. Secret, discreet or official, abortion is practiced everywhere. In South America or Africa abortion is not legal, but it does exist: it's important not to show it or talk about it – no advertising, please! Women in these countries urge us not to speak but to do.

In the end, partly as a result of these strategic errors, the International Women's Health Coalition disappeared as an entity and joined another association, West Planned Parenthood.

I also joined the Women's Commission for Refugee Women and Children, an organisation founded by my good friend Mary Anne Schwalbe, who fought for this cause from Thailand to Afghanistan. She succumbed to pancreatic cancer, the same disease that struck the young woman who headed the Commission's office in the Philippines. I've always wondered whether the total commitment of both of them didn't end up devouring them.

When the organisation celebrated its thirtieth anniversary in New York recently, Mary Anne's name wasn't even mentioned in the speeches – the founder, forgotten. I protested, but to no avail – the memory is so evanescent! A cruel lesson: in associations, everyone tries to erase the memory of their predecessors. Don't we always want to appear alone, powerful and generous at the same time? Yes, egos are paramount in NGOs! In principle there's no money in it: you may be handling money, but it's for others, you're not getting rich. So what's left? Ego!

As you can see, in the land of NGOs all is not always rosy and easy. I was on the UK board of the International Rescue Committee headed in New York by the Englishman David Miliband, a close friend of former Prime Minister Tony Blair, then one of the leading figures of the young Labour generation and perhaps a future British Prime Minister. It wasn't just a grassroots NGO, but rather an international organisation whose aim was to change laws through political lobbying. In the US our influence was limited, but we worked with lawyers on abortion rights issues in Canada.

I also went to Sierra Leone with this association... and I discovered how absurdity and renunciation could sometimes limit action, even though it was essential. We had to run a rape crisis centre, the Rape Crisis Committee. When we arrived at the centre, which was run by six employees, there were four cases of rape that day, including a four-year-old and a fourteen-year-old. The banality of everyday life, alas.

The teenager was pregnant, and I suggested that she be offered an abortion as soon as possible. 'Impossible, abortion is illegal,' I was told coldly. 'But we can't abandon this little girl…' The association's representatives gave me a definitive answer without appeal: 'There's nothing we can do. We receive subsidies from the American government, and we absolutely cannot encourage a young woman to have an abortion.'

I proposed several solutions, including acting personally to send the young woman to a medical centre. Inconceivably, my membership of the International Rescue Committee ruled out all my suggestions.

'So, what are you going to do? You're going to let a fourteen-year-old have a child?'

How could I accept an anti-rape programme so frosty and so limited? When I got back to London, I reported on what I'd seen, explained my positions, expressed my indignation, and finally resigned.

In Madagascar, I think it's even worse, because of endemic corruption, the aid doesn't go to those who really need it. There was a whole programme on the island to install solar panels that would produce electricity and bring light to the villages. A laudable intention, but nobody came to check where and how these famous solar panels were installed, and the electricity still hasn't reached the villages! Similarly, I've seen Malagasy hospitals paid for by international aid… completely empty! The rare patients are wealthy islanders willing to pay dearly for treatment. All too often, NGOs simply raise the money, but no one checks the results and watches out for possible abuses.

Some of the organisations I've seen at work in Africa seemed outdated at times, and should be renewed. They did admirable work thirty years ago, and then the world around them changed, and needs evolved. I think that any NGO should close down after twenty-five years of activity. If mine doesn't close down, I make sure that it constantly renews its missions. George Soros, president of the Soros Fund Management, explained that after too many years of action the survival of the organisation becomes more important than the work it does. He's right; I've seen it so often.

First, members must not stay with an association for too long; secondly, the vision must be regularly adapted to changing circumstances. In some African countries circumstances have changed for many women. Here and there African women have acquired some power, and associations must take that into account or they can no longer play their role.

African women are extraordinary, fantastic, funny, warm and wonderful. I'm thinking in particular of Sister Venita, a nun from Cameroon who officiates in Sierra Leone. She belongs to the Sisters of the Holy Cross of Jerusalem. With her congregation she looks after almost a thousand girls, to whom she strives to provide a regular education. In 2013, during the Ebola epidemic, I asked her what she needed.

'Chlorine,' she replied.

She disinfected the entire school, water circuits, classrooms and corridors. The happy result: she didn't lose a single pupil. I thought then that all the international organisations and dozens of NGOs working in Africa should have done the same thing. It was elementary. Sometimes you're stunned by the carelessness, clumsiness and indifference…

Later, Sister Venita came to New York and stayed with me.

'Would you like to see a Broadway show?' I asked her. I took her to see *South Pacific*, a classic musical comedy, and then took her to dinner at a Broadway restaurant. Dazzled, she discovered a world that was totally unknown to her. 'I think I'm in heaven,' she confided.

This furtive discovery of an earthly paradise didn't stop her from getting up at 5 a.m. the next morning to say her prayers.

More recently she has benefitted from a university

scholarship in Florida and has just obtained a master's degree in mental health.

In Madagascar, it is the Good Shepherd Sisters who help a population that is sometimes at a loss, working in particular with prostitutes. They give them condoms, because they know that these women won't stop selling their bodies, but at least that prevents them from catching AIDS. That, for me, is the Catholic Church going in the right direction, that of pragmatism and generosity.

But it's not just in developing countries that we've been active. With our American foundation we supported six girls from ethnic minorities, two African-American, two Indian and two Hispanic. We enabled them to follow a high-level course of study, normally inaccessible given their social condition. All six succeeded brilliantly. Sandy, for example, came from an African American family, where out of five children she was the only one to finish her standard education. She was accepted at Yale and then at the University of Pennsylvania, where she obtained a doctorate and is now pursuing a brilliant career. Another went to the University of St Andrews in Scotland, and became a chemist. As for the two Indian young women originally from Punjab, both have made successful careers in technology and one of them sits on the Global Foundation for Humanity board.

One of the two Hispanics, the one I followed most closely, came from an extremely difficult background, but had amazed her teachers with her sharp intelligence, and had been taken on by an organisation in Harlem, the Center for Child Development. This Center, founded by Kenneth B. Clark, a leading African-American sociologist, took care of children. First of all, there were 'crack babies', born to mothers addicted to crack cocaine. Then children with serious problems, particularly psychological, were taken in. My friend the philanthropist Susan Patricof, who supported the Center, brought a young pupil to my attention. The idea was to get her out of the Center and into Marymount, a private Catholic school in New York, which had invited me to join its Board of Directors.

'We have this fourteen-year-old girl. She's fantastic, but she has a lot of problems.'

I consulted Marymount's principal, Sister Kathleen: 'Will you come with me to meet this young girl?

We went. The teenager was accepted, a courageous decision as she struggled with her studies. But Marymount took good care of her and in the end she went on to study at university, succeeded brilliantly, and worked in a bank where she had a high-level job. She married, and had two children. And then, at the age of thirty-four, she decided to give up her career in finance to become a nurse. She wanted to give back to society all the good it had given her.

A fine American story, which seems to me to correspond perfectly with what's happening over there. When President Biden was inaugurated minorities came to the fore, led by Vice President Kamala Harris, half-Indian, half-African American and a woman. Another woman, Hispanic Supreme Court Justice Sonia Sotomayor, took the oath of office from the newly elected president.

Such is the America of today. Minorities are beginning to take their place and will contribute enormously to the country's development, I'm convinced.

I still remember Judith Lichtman, an effective lawyer at the head of the Washington-based Women's Legal Defense Fund; Mahmoud Fathallah, an Egyptian obstetrician, a great ally of the women's cause; Aryeh Neier, co-founder of Human Rights Watch, for the universal defence of human rights. Today I appreciate the luck I had to cross paths with these brilliant and generous minds.

The kaleidoscope of these experiences, these actions carried out as nearby as possible or at the other end of the world, shows different aspects of reality, certainly, but in the end women's problems always remain the same. In South America, Africa and Asia the issues are recurrent: women are exploited, bullied and abused.

The Sustainable Development Agenda, adopted by UN member states in 2015, set a deadline of 2030 for the achievement of gender equality and the empowerment of all women. Today, with less than ten years left to achieve this, the world is not on track. According to the UN, countries must ensure universal and equal access to quality, inclusive and equitable education and learning, which must be free and compulsory, leaving no one behind, regardless of gender, disability, social and economic status. Education must aim at the full development of the human personality, and promote mutual understanding, tolerance, friendship and peace. Education must go beyond basic literacy and numeracy skills, and equip individuals with creative, critical thinking and collaborative skills, while developing curiosity, courage and resilience. Education is a public good.

Progress in gender equality has stagnated and even begun to reverse! According to UNESCO in 2024, 122 million girls in the world are not in school. Everywhere, women's rights are increasingly flouted, threatening even well-established freedoms and protections.

What can we do? Keep on fighting, keep on speaking out. And every era raises its own set of problems and provokes new indignation. The State of World Population Report 2020, published by the United Nations Population Fund, estimates that 140 million women are missing from planet Earth. Not that these millions of women have just gone off on some intergalactic jaunt; simply, they are tragically missing at birth.

Confirming this appalling statistic, a study by the King Abdullah University of Science and Technology in Jeddah, published in August 2021 by the *British Medical Journal*, predicts that men will outnumber women by 2100 – with an additional 5.7 million missing female births between 2022 and 2100!

The cause of this disparity? Some societies continue to favour boys over girls. The advent of readily available sex-identification technology has led to the widespread abortion of female foetuses, leading to a worldwide increase of 25 per cent in male births since the 1990s.

Prior to this, female infants were frequently victims of death or neglect, and in some cases still are. Research published by *The Lancet* on 8 April 2021 focuses on birth trends in India, which accounts for half of the world's missing female births: these 'totalled around 30 million between 1980 and 2010'. The authors announced that 'without reductions in sex-selective abortion, the profound demographic and social repercussions of missing girls will continue'. A society without enough women leads to more violence against women, more trafficking in women, more organised crime, more geopolitical instability, more wars.

In many societies boys are still favoured for socio-economic and cultural reasons. If a woman is pregnant with a baby girl she may be forced to have an abortion. If she refuses, she will face violence, rejection by her family, and, in some cases, death. Girls are discriminated against because they are seen as a financial burden, requiring a dowry in some countries, and allegedly unable to provide for their own families financially. As they say in India, 'Raising a daughter is like watering your neighbour's garden.'

Only three countries have successfully tackled the gender imbalance: South Korea, Georgia and Hong Kong. In South Korea, for example, the acute imbalance between men and women thrived until the 1990s, when it was corrected through a combination of education and legislation, showing the rest of the world that it is possible to fight deeply rooted societal prejudices.

While legislation on inheritance and land ownership guaranteeing gender equity is one way of combating discrimination, the most powerful weapon of all is education. Educating women effectively increases their value in the eyes of their own societies, and reduces family size. How then can we fail to mention Malala Yousafzai, the famous Pakistani activist? At the World Education Summit held in London in July 2021 the young woman exclaimed: 'If we want a stronger, fairer world we must keep girls learning.'

I realise that in the current global education crisis this simple idea is not going to be easy to implement. But educating girls improves public health, mitigates climate change, promotes peace, supports economic growth. Yes, the education of girls leads us collectively towards a fairer, more peaceful world.

IV
Why India?

Everything comes to us that belongs to us
if we create the capacity to receive it.
Rabindranath Tagore

In 1993 I founded what came to be known as the Veerni Project, aimed at helping young Indian women in the remote Thar Desert of Rajasthan. It was India that chose me, India that captivated me. India, a multiple, ever-changing country, a country as amazing as it is fantastic, a country of all ethnic groups. From the mountainous north to the tropical south, Indians are diverse, always surprising, always fascinating. Different peoples, different languages, different faiths... Isn't Hinduism the only religion that doesn't claim to hold the Truth? There is no single god who represents the only certainty, the only evidence, as in our religions. India is thus the land of all truths. In fact, you only have to approach the Ganges to understand. Some 100,000 deities are worshipped on the river! Isn't Hinduism said to be the religion of 33 million gods?

In the West we tend too much to believe in one Truth, whereas India teaches us that there are, on the contrary, many truths. In London I had a great friend, a wonderful person, the philosopher Isaiah Berlin. He taught me that democracy may be an imperfect institution, but it's the only one in which we can live: it avoids the risk of power being seized by those who claim to hold the truth! India, the land of multiple truths, changed me radically from the Catholicism I grew up with in Fribourg.

India, the land of multiple truths, should therefore escape

fanaticism. It's true that for a long time Hindus, Muslims, Buddhists and Christians evolved peacefully side by side. Unfortunately, for political reasons, the situation has become tense, and coexistence is now in danger.

What also fascinates me about India is its attitude to death. Death is omnipresent, and we are constantly exposed to it. Back home we hide death, we don't know how to deal with it. In India the dead are accompanied for twelve days and nights: we don't part from them at once. The men are outside, the women stand by the body, and we weep for twelve days… And then it's over. Life goes on.

As I said, India has little in common with the Fribourg of my childhood, but the perception of death is similar. I grew up in a house where the dead were laid out in the living room, so I was exposed to death. It was sinister, perhaps, but we used to pray around the open coffin – my grandmother's, and later my father's.

My children's generation, on the other hand, has never faced death. Now we don't deal well with the end of life: people die in hospitals in an antiseptic and anonymous world; we no longer die at home surrounded by our family…

India teaches us tolerance, but also the importance of rivers and the value of water as a source of life. It is quite extraordinary that the two most populous countries on the planet are located north and south of the Himalayas. There are 2.8 billion people living and evolving on either side of the same mountain range! Development has occurred thanks to the rivers that spring from it. The origin of our survival is water, water that comes from the heights – the Himalayas there, the Alps in Europe.

India and China… ancient civilisations, peoples who built, wrote, created and thought, when we were still barbarians! I love India, but modern China terrifies me with its state control. I went to China for the first time in 1984, and it was a terribly poor country compared to today. India hasn't made that leap;

basic human problems are hard to solve in a democracy. India hasn't managed to solve basic problems because the country is chaotic. Chaos, yes, but in which there is a certain order, that of compassion and freedom. In India you can move about, you can go and work in another state, you have a human freedom that you clearly don't find in China. But China has agreed to educate its girls, something India is still reluctant to do. And if you refuse to educate half the population, progress will obviously be more arduous.

Dictatorial China solved problems that India still faces, but the Chinese of the third millennium are a people without a collective memory. By contrast – and this is part of what appeals to me – India's collective memory is very strong. The *Bhagavad Gita*, the 'Song of God', one of the basic writings of Hinduism, an extraordinary, richly layered narrative written perhaps two and a half thousand years ago, still speaks to us. It tells the story of Arjuna, a warrior prince who hesitates to engage in battle because members of his family are in the enemy army.

The difficulty of India's evolution was summed up for me by an old sage who looked after beehives in a village in Provence: 'India is the land of ants,' he explained. 'If you're a worker, you will be a worker for the rest of your life. The United States, on the other hand, is the land of bees: you can start out as a worker and end up as a queen.'

To act in India is always to want to fight against the imposed evidence, so that the ant doesn't remain an ant.

At international conferences I was soon faced with the basic problem of reproductive rights. This rather inelegant and imprecise term in fact covers everything to do with women's health. And it is true that women's intimate lives call for specific medical attention. In India in the early 1990s I discovered a subcontinent where women had no rights, no control over their fertility. There was no access to knowledge and no consideration of women's lives. At the age of fifty an Indian woman, and especially a poor Indian woman, ceased to exist: nothing more was thought about for her. She no longer had children, so she was cast aside! No programme existed to help women throughout their lives. A woman's existence is a whole that implies the ability to make essential life choices: access to education, a profession, financial independence, marriage, children... But first and foremost a woman has the right to health. Without health she can do nothing.

With the help of my former husband Robert Towbin, we set up the Global Foundation for Humanity in the United States in 1993. The mission of the Foundation was women and girls' empowerment through health and education. Along with the creation of Veerni, we gave scholarships to minority girls in New York to go to elite private schools far removed from public schools with metal detectors. Six of them benefitted from the Foundation – three young Indian women, two African-American and one Hispanic. They went on to college, some to graduate school, and five have good careers. Two of them are full professors, one is a neurologist, another one is in a successful job and sits on the board of the Global Foundation for Humanity and is involved in Veerni, the other one is a successful Uber driver married with two children. In all these cases a good education transformed their lives, and we have kept in touch with most of them. I wish to take this occasion to thank the wonderful board of the Global Foundation in our pioneer years who gave so much support and wisdom. We could not have done it without them.

The Veerni Project began with the aim of bringing reproductive health services to poor women in the villages of Rajasthan, between Jodhpur (where it was established) and Pakistan, one of the poorest regions in the world, a difficult land where agriculture depends entirely on the monsoon, with rudimentary houses, very few public services at the time, torrid temperatures in summer, freezing in winter… Our entry point was the health of the child and the mother. Why did we do this? Because the villages were so closed, so hostile to any outside influence, that reaching the women was going to be difficult. If we targeted the women through their children the men felt less threatened. At first, we had no access to women. On our first adventures into the villages, we weren't really welcome. On some occasions men even pretended to stone us. But little by little we gained the villagers' trust and proved to them that we weren't just another project that arrived for a short period and soon disappeared. We were here for the long haul! Too many associations have come to India, drawn up more or less well-thought-out projects, stayed on for a few months or years, and then disappeared, no doubt to take shape as another project elsewhere. But nothing good or solid can be achieved without long-term commitment.

I remember one of my first visits to a totally isolated village in the Thar Desert. At the request of the villagers, we provided sewing lessons. To set up this practical teaching programme we organised a 7 a.m. meeting with the villagers. We arrived… there were only men sitting in a circle waiting for us, and the women were standing far behind. I said: 'Look, this programme is for women, so they need to be part of the conversation.'

Movement. The women stepped forward. But the men still wanted to impose their views. 'We want sewing centres for our women, but you're not allowed to talk to them about health or contraception…'

Very diplomatically I thanked the men for their concerns and suggested that we should keep listening to the women.

When I returned to the village six months later, they had indeed responded to the women's wishes: a volunteer Canadian nurse was giving a lesson on contraception and demonstrating how to use a condom.

So, I thought, this is what India is all about: you start with impossibilities, you set up prohibitions, and a few months later everything has evolved, everything has changed. You have to take things one step at a time, listen to the wisdom of women who have so little power because their mother-in-law – their husband's mother – is in charge. I had to distract the mother-in-law so many times, keep her busy, take her elsewhere, while the nurse inserted an IUD in her daughter-in-law, who secretly didn't want any more children.

So there was contraception... but also AIDS, alas. A devastating, ghastly disease! All too often I took sick people to hospital, but they died in front of me; there was nothing we could do. The epidemic was like an unstoppable wave, spread especially by truck drivers and men who went to work in the city. Prostitutes worked on Indian roads and everywhere in the big cities; the men returned to the village, and without knowing it contaminated their wives. Whole families were reduced: father and mother died, leaving behind young children. In just one of these villages in the Thar Desert we had to take in three orphans.

We spotted cases of AIDS before the government recognised the problem and took steps to combat the epidemic. Sadly, several young women succumbed – it was too late for them. With time, and thanks to Veerni's remarkable doctor, Dr Joshi, the Government Hospital in Jodhpur finally set up an AIDS programme. We were able to help many patients who are alive today and have access to the necessary medication. Once adopted, the treatment programmes were applied, but prevention was not effective enough, largely due to the limitation of contraception methods.

One day in a village I found a half-dead woman on the side of the road. The family believed her to be possessed by a demon and a priest had burned her three times on the stomach with a red-hot iron – atrocious scars! Our ambulance immediately took her to Jodhpur's main hospital. The doctors confirmed that this young woman had indeed contracted AIDS, and she was stabilized. Today

The Veerni staff

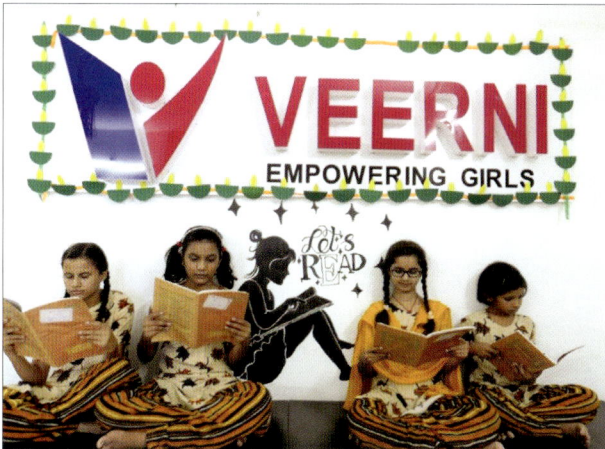

Room to read

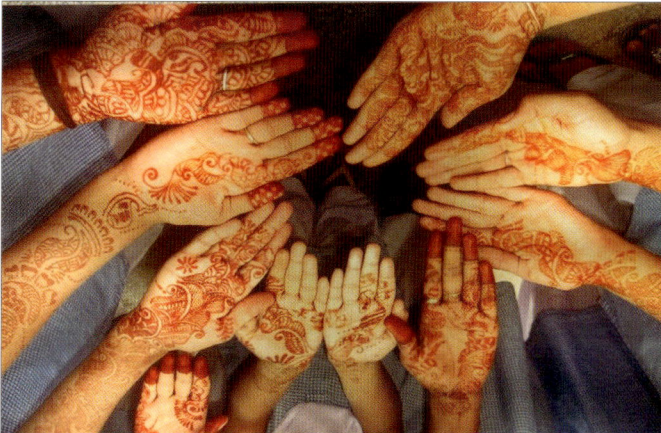

Rangoli, symbol of happiness and good luck

Meeting with village women

Village meeting about child brides

Group photo

Veerni dorm

Veerni girls

Power walk

Durga's parents (Veerni girl)

Future Veerni girls

Group outing

Village Veerni representatives

Lecture in the institute

His Highness the Maharajah of Jodhpur and Jacqueline de Chollet

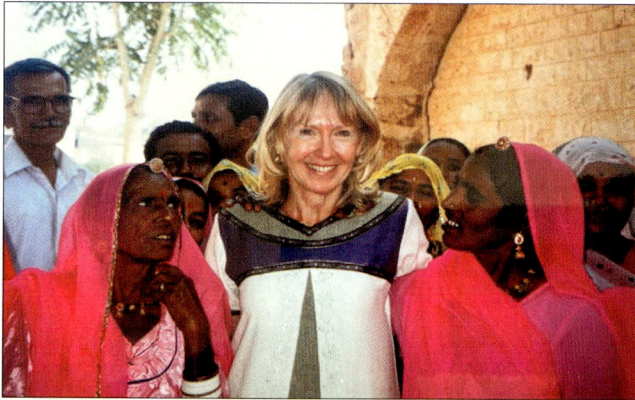

Jacqueline and Veerni village representatives

HRH the Duchess of Cornwall & Her Highness Maharani Sahiba
interacting with the child brides studying at the Veerni Institute

Daily sports

Girls' determination and courage

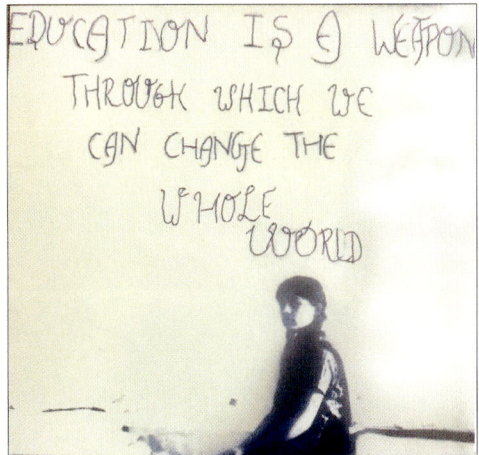

Veerni motivation

Sophie with the girls

Fun times

Women in purdah

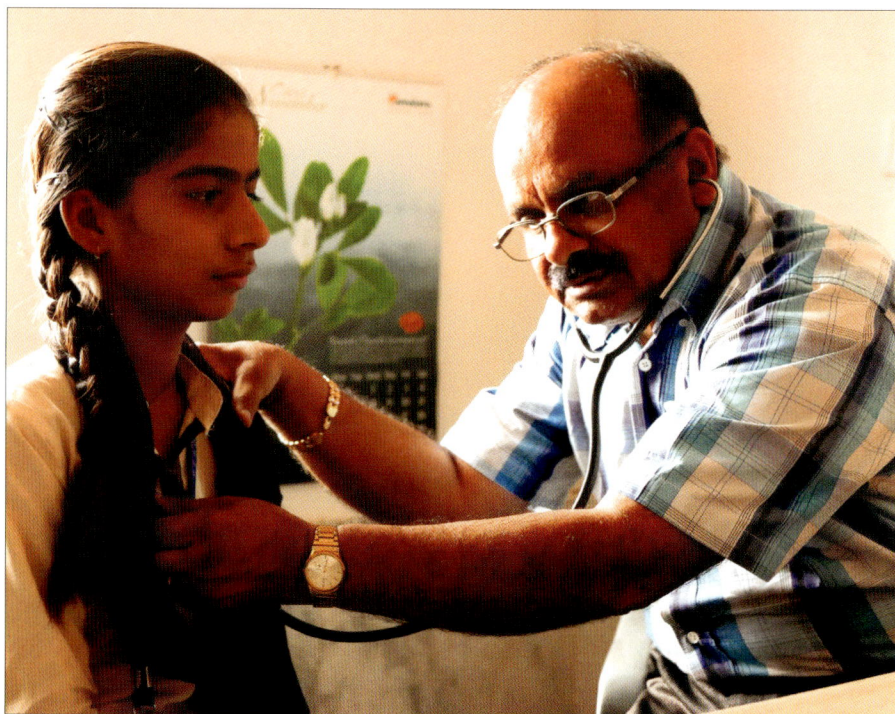
Veerni medical

she is still under treatment, but is doing well. The overworked, exhausted doctors, always working in Dantesque hospitals, saved her life. In my eyes, they are true heroes.

Fortunately, the AIDS epidemic is no longer so virulent. India was one of the first countries to develop affordable antiretroviral drugs for itself and others. The government set up treatment centres through NACO, the National AIDS Control Organisation, and information on the subject has spread. All this, combined with treatment, has helped curb the disease, though not to make it disappear.

Yet for a long time AIDS programmes were sometimes inadequate. In Kerala, in the south, information was spread, but in Rajasthan, in the north, action stalled. The cause: backward mentalities and a widely dispersed rural population. Villages remain outside the mainstream because there is little investment from central government. Besides, what's the point of investing? The men migrate to the cities, leaving the women alone and vulnerable. It's true that the situation has improved considerably. While AIDS has not disappeared, the disease is controllable.

Public health remains a fundamental problem in some Indian states. We have discovered problems that we had not suspected. Cataracts are one of them! In the Thar Desert this condition is one of the most aggressive in the world, due to the lack of prevention and the virulence of the sunlight, caused by the reverberation caused by the lack of vegetation. Sandstorms and lack of sunglasses add to the risk of cataracts. Even today the so-called 'lower' castes are not allowed to wear dark glasses, as this would be considered a total lack of respect towards the 'higher' castes!

Through an American friend, the major lens company Bausch & Lomb offered us a thousand lenses to treat cataracts. We set up an agreement with the Tarabai Desai Eye Hospital in Jodhpur: given the thousand lenses, surgeons there agreed to operate free of charge on some hundred villagers suffering from cataracts. It was a fruitful cooperation for all concerned. They had the lenses – the best – and some patients were able to see again!

We drove the villagers to Jodhpur for the operation, which took place at night to avoid the heat and dust. I witnessed some of these operations myself: two Desai brothers operated all night long using state-of-the-art machines, and probably treated more cases in one night than some ophthalmologists do in a week back home! With this they not only restored sight but also gave a new lease of life to people in our villages who without this action risked losing the ability to work and sinking into poverty. What's more, it gave the Veerni Project a good reputation for helping the elderly, who are always respected in their families.

The good will was welcome, because women's health was particularly important to us. The general lack of interest in this issue, a shameful neglect, remained a constant concern for us. Anemia, a major problem especially for women of childbearing age, was one of the main causes of maternal mortality. This widespread anemia was due to discrimination against women from birth onwards, and the scant nourishment they received. Indeed, women and girls were fed last… after men and boys!

In India overall the prevalence of anemia is 52 per cent, and it is higher still in Rajasthan due to poverty, often deficient food resources, and irregular harvests. Yet the only Indian government programme for pregnant women at the time was the distribution of iron tablets, which were generally poorly tolerated, hence ineffective. These iron tablets are not easy to digest, and cause women severe stomach pains. And yet they have never been modified, and it's not uncommon to see boxes piling up in health centres, undistributed and unused. Fortunately, we have distributed another type of iron supplement, which is much better tolerated.

With Shirley Johnson-Lans, Professor of Health Economics at Vassar University in the USA, Veerni set up a research project on anemia involving five hundred women and as many teenage girls, in order to establish programmes to prevent and cure anemia. We had to convince the village women to give intravenous blood: they were reluctant at first, convinced that we were taking blood from them to sell.

When the research project started in 2006, the level of anemia was 76 per cent among teenage girls and 81 per cent among adult women, with varying degrees, but with the percentage of severe anemia reaching almost 3 per cent. I saw a woman ready to give birth with a haemoglobin level of 3 whereas the normal degree is 12 in the West and 11 in India.

According to an Indian family health survey between 2019 and 2021 a growing number of people are affected by anemia, and this applies to all population groups, including children under five, teenage girls, young boys, and pregnant women. It is therefore essential to assess anemia, as it can present a risk of complications during pregnancy, premature delivery, or low birth weight. It can also pose a threat to the mother through the potential for blood loss during labour, making it more difficult for the body to fight off infections.

Cervical cancer kills more women in India than anywhere else, and women die of breast cancer at the age of thirty. In the West girls are vaccinated against cervical cancer, but not in India, because no one is looking after women's health. Every year 67,000 Indian women succumb to this form of cancer! In the countryside there is little screening and no health policy, as if the rural world had been abandoned.

In India there is an urban country and a rural country. These two Indians live side by side without ever meeting. The Indians I know in the cities have access to information and education, and never set foot in a village; in urban India girls are educated. Rural India is often in the Middle Ages, cruelly lacking in care and information. Indeed, to modernise India, wouldn't it be necessary to build many small towns equipped with efficient public services? A presumptuous dream, because everything depends on the states, and the rich advance while the poor stagnate.

As we have seen, Kerala is enjoying a certain degree of prosperity, and history can explain this success. In the nineteenth-century Catholic missionaries went there and educated young people, including girls. So, Kerala doesn't need the help of people like me: the missionaries had already invested in education, and had done so for a long time. Rajasthan, on the other hand, is in a region that is fully Hindu, and a little Muslim, where investment in women's future has always been inadequate. And that makes all the difference. In Rajasthan 60 per cent of women are still illiterate. One of them said to me: 'How can I take a bus if I can't read where it's going?'

Did you know that only 22 per cent of Indian women work? Among international bodies India is the country with the fewest women involved in administration – along with Saudi Arabia.

According to the Global Gender Gap Index, published by the World Economic Forum, in 2022 India still ranked 135th out of 146 countries in terms of gender equality. Involving women in development in India would increase the country's GDP by 27 per cent.

Where was I headed when I founded a project to help young Indian women? I didn't know which paths would lead me there, but I knew that the goal was education. To achieve this, I had to make many contacts, approach many offices, and meet many autocrats!

We organised sewing centres and distributed dozens of sewing machines, providing a way for women not only to work for their families but also to earn a little money. We had a centre in Jodhpur where we brought the women in once a week; we organised transport, taught them the art of sewing, and then sold their work for them.

Programmes were established well: a baby programme, a hygiene programme, a contraception programme. Each day of the week had its own calling.

During that period, I was accompanied by Anne Vincent who first visited India with me in 1993. She played a crucial rose in developing sewing programmes that provided income for village women. She became an integral part of Veerni for many years.

To develop our activities, we had promoters in every village – thirty-five in all. They were usually women who represented their village for us and wore a pink uniform – the colour of the Veerni Project, and of power in Rajasthan. We also had male promoters, because we always had to work with men to explain our actions to them. With these promoters and representatives of the Trust of the Maharaja of Jodhpur, the all-powerful figure in the region on whom we depended at the time, we held monthly meetings in our administrative centre. Women were on one side, men on the other, and the leaders sat on their chairs.

'Either we all sit on the floor or we give everyone chairs,' I said. They chose chairs for everyone! The handsome gentlemen didn't want to get their precious clothes dirty.

Since the women were sitting on chairs they could easily get up and speak, and as a result they were put on an equal footing. In a sudden psychological shift, they now spoke out loud and clear.

These projects enabled some of the women to learn to read and write, and some even became members of their *panchayat*, the village administration. In India a law requires *panchayats* to have at least 30 per cent female members. So, they were there, but they were illiterate and did nothing. With us, the women took their rightful place. One of our students was even put in charge of her *panchayat*! It is remarkable how quickly they adapted.

Progress is being made. For example, since the 2010s pregnant women have been paid by the Indian government to give birth in hospitals, which has significantly reduced maternal mortality. But there is still the problem of transport to the hospital from remote desert villages, where there are no roads for vehicles. Women end up on scooters, tractors, buffalo carts or any other means available, all of which are dangerous for a pregnant woman.

At the Veerni Project headquarters in Jodhpur we created 'safe delivery kits' for midwives. What is in the kit? Clean string for the umbilical cord, a new razor blade to cut the cord instead of a rusty old one, a plastic sheet to prevent the woman giving birth on contaminated sand, soap, plastic gloves, and finally a clean towel to wrap the newborn. These basic things save lives!

Alongside the kits we set up nutrition programmes. Poverty, discrimination against women, and a lack of important elements in food, especially proteins, led to numerous deficiencies. The vast majority of children in the villages monitored by Veerni were malnourished. With the help of Antenna, an international organisation founded by a Swiss, Denis von der Weid, we set up campaigns of spirulina, a supplement that contains many essential vitamins. Veerni has also worked with an Ayurvedic centre to produce nourishing soy-based biscuits to improve children's diets.

V

The Goal: Education

The future of our world is
only as bright as our girls.
Michelle Obama

There have been many changes and good developments since we first set foot in India. Over the years there have been discussions, good meetings, dramas avoided, great surprises... I'm thinking of 8 March 1996. On that day the women put down their tools and announced to their husbands that they were not going to work in the house or in the fields: they were all celebrating International Women's Day together! A cultural programme was even organised in which the women sang traditional songs together, and young girls put on song and dance shows. A few years earlier such an event would have been completely impossible. For me this celebration was a real wonder. How did these women even know that 8 March was Women's Day? They had so little contact with the outside world, no access to electricity, television or newspapers, and so many of them were illiterate. And yet they did it! It was a day of triumph for Veerni.

Today life has changed in the villages where we are present, not only for many women but also for teenage girls. Over the years Veerni has focused on secondary education for girls, and the results have been gratifying. Around 90 per cent of our girls have gone on to higher education. And this education leads to a profession, a guarantee of independence...

Crucially, however, access to a profession – however necessary that profession may be – is not the only feature of a well-managed education. An educated young woman may first gain access to health, and she will also be able to make her own decisions about how to lead her life as a woman. She may choose to lead a life other than the traditional one of housewife. And if she marries, she will resist pressure to choose the sex of her first child in order to have a son, and she will freely decide on the number of children and how to raise them.

In the West we are used to judging success by income and position. I think there are other measures of success, and young Western women are beginning to realise this. It is not just a matter of material success: it is also about living your dream, contributing to society, having a richer life. When the inner person is just as important as the outer person there is balance, but if the measure of outer success is too high the inner person will suffer. The difference? Outer success is based on position and income; the inner person wants to do good and understand others… This fusion of the two sides of our personality is essential to our wholeness: I believe that the balance between these two parts of our nature is the key to a fairer, more caring society.

In India as elsewhere I truly believe that women's abilities and contribution to society are not limited to bearing children and cooking! I think society needs to look beyond that role assigned to many women and consider women's contribution in all areas. There have been some very powerful Indian women and their role in the country has been very important, as we know. Today India needs more active women, and Veerni is training some of them. They are the future leaders.

Inspired by the words of the Indian economist and philosopher Amartya Sen, Veerni sees young women as agents of social transformation who must take their rightful place in society. Without education this cannot happen. I know that Veerni girls will have the ability to change their parents' vision.

They will have what young Western women already have: access to a bank account, a telephone, control over their lives; they will be able to acquire economic independence and with that earn the respect of their communities.

Veerni's aim has been and remains the development of women in the modern world and for the modern world. These women will contribute to the life of their country in every possible way. In this development a country like India can make the most of this choice: women's contribution can be immeasurable and decisive. Yes, young women can transform society.

So, if the world is serious about secondary education for young women it needs to make a long-term and urgent commitment to more egalitarian and inclusive societies. In short, girls' education must be at the forefront of all international agendas.

Indeed, secondary education should be a priority throughout the world; it is one of the United Nations' sustainable development goals. We know that the majority of the world's un-schooled children are girls. In the desert region of Rajasthan boys go to school but not girls. There used to be a local saying that 'girls are made for marriage, not education'. As a result, rural India fails to educate the majority of its girls, especially as secondary schools are few and far between and often of mediocre quality, with teachers forgetting to come for days at a time in favour of more profitable tasks. What's more, for young girls the ever-present risk of rape makes it dangerous to walk several kilometres through the desert to get to school: the question of safety remains a major problem. For too many, girls' education stops at the age of twelve, at the end of elementary school, even though they are obviously not fully educated at that age.

Once school is over, many girls never open a book, and forget what they've learned. If women remain illiterate, how can they take their rightful place in society, in the political life of their country, and play a role in the life of their communities?

In the Veerni Project the girls live in an institute in Jodhpur, where we give them the opportunity to attend excellent private schools. They graduate, and can continue their studies in literature, business or science, which open many doors for them. The majority do go on to higher education, including the precociously married teenagers who sometimes make up half of our boarders. Luckily parents don't usually force these girls to join their husbands, and they are allowed to continue studying for a few years. In some rare cases their marriages are even annulled, which represents a clear advance in attitudes.

Child marriage has officially been illegal in India since 1939. Nevertheless, the practice is deeply rooted in the culture of many rural areas, and parents marry off their children in secret. According to UNICEF almost half of Indian women were married by the age of eighteen, and nearly one in five was married before the age of fifteen. India alone accounts for around a third of child marriages worldwide.

Protected at Veerni, our girls learn to think for themselves and are able to take a sharp look at their lives, their society and their families. They talk, tell their story, and even make their lives the subject of plays that they perform at our Institute. The marriage of girl children, the relationship with the mother-in-law, the unknown husband, contraception... They present all this with keenness and talent!

One of the most impoverished villages that we helped was home entirely to Dalits, the so-called 'untouchables'. In this village all the little girls used to be married off very young! Radical change: in 2016 the village announced that the custom of early marriage was abolished. It was a momentous decision for a community of Dalits. Today the value of their daughters' education is recognised, and these children are given the chance to become economically productive and to marry better husbands.

Because of the asymmetrical sex ratio there are fewer girls in these regions, and this is a real concern. An educated girl is now a valuable asset, and her ability to improve her life and make her own choices has become a reality. Hillary Clinton said: 'There cannot be true democracy unless women's voices are heard. There cannot be true democracy unless women are given the opportunity to take responsibility for their own lives.'

All together, we must work to ensure that all women and girls have what we take for granted in the West. We need to understand that the world will never be a better place if women are marginalised, treated as second-class citizens, or worse, as a commodity that men can dispose of. As long as we talk about women's empowerment but don't act on it, their fate will make little progress.

What does empowerment mean? The ability for a woman to make her own choices. Too many women around the world are denied this opportunity. There will be no social transformation in any country if women remain outside the decision-making bodies that affect the lives of their families, their communities and their countries. Let's work together to bring about the changes that will guarantee autonomy, freedom and education for women the world over. Then the world will be a better place. For me, investment in the future is done by women's education.

In India schools are the responsibility of the government, but there are many private schools, and our girls go to these schools, which are excellent. They are better than government schools for girls because they offer students broader fields of knowledge, especially in scientific studies and business. Without this range, career opportunities for women would be more limited.

What is this woman doing in India? What is she looking for? Why does she come back month after month? These were the questions that Indians of all castes and backgrounds asked themselves as I wandered through the remote villages of

Rajasthan. They couldn't understand why a Western woman would do something in their country that they themselves wouldn't do. Faced with this absolute mystery, they didn't know how to treat the strange foreigner. Where should she be placed in the rigorous Indian hierarchy? For example, in Indian marriages women were placed on one side and men on the other, but I had the right to go to the men's side as well as the women's, because I was in a way in a class of my own, a *memsaab*, a woman of authority.

In fact, I benefitted greatly from this intermediary position, as it enabled me to place myself on both sides of society – that of the poor in order to understand them, and that of those in power in order to defend the poor. But it took a great deal of psychology to know how to talk, subtly bring up subjects, always thank the authorities – for what they didn't do!

'I know you've really tried, you care about poor people, and of course I'm sure you would like to see things change…'

The more we thanked them for what they weren't doing, the more we put them in a position to do something!

Our work was helped greatly by His Highness the Maharaja of Jodhpur, a good friend of mine. I had met Gaj Singh, nicknamed Bapji, with my second husband, the viscount. We had gone on vacation to India with all our children, toured the country, and arrived in Jodhpur. Our hotel was in a wing of the Umaid Bhawan palace. When the Maharaja was told that Viscount and Viscountess Weir were within the walls, he immediately invited us to dine at his table with our children, then to lunch, then to walk with him around his grounds…

Almost ten years later I was no longer a viscountess; I was divorced, but I still got back in touch with Bapji. He helped us with great kindness and sincere commitment, and we owe him a great deal. Here is how he agreed to present and support the Veerni Project: 'It's encouraging to learn that the girls have done well academically, as well as in sports and extracurricular activities. We can see the change in the girls' overall personalities: shy, weak and somewhat withdrawn, they are now confident and self-assured.'

Since 1999 we have been protected by the Trust of the Maharaja of Jodhpur. Under the leadership of the Trust's Director-cum-Coordinator who became Director of the Veerni Project as well, a brigadier by the name of Shakti Singh, who had experience of village life, we were able to make progress and expand the project to two vehicles and a resident doctor. But not without some tension at first, because the men's style was authoritarian. I was led to say to the director and the doctor:

'Gentlemen, your management style is somewhat intimidating for a woman, a project for women, largely run by women in the field, and funded by women.'

'We're two sixty-five-year-old men and we can't change,' they replied, 'I'm a sixty-year-old woman and I myself can't change. So what are we going to do?' I asked. It was all in good humour!

One day, on the way to a conference far away in the desert on a narrow track, the doctor was driving Indian style at 90 miles an hour and I was terrified in the back seat. So I told him, 'You know my husband is a powerful man in the US, and if something happens to me because of your driving he is going to come after you.' He slowed down – a little.

However, their style softened. We were no longer part of the Indian Army! We will be always grateful to Brigadier Singh for his leadership and all the time he gave the Project. He also became a great friend.

In October 2010 Prince Charles and Camilla, Duchess of Cornwall, were in Jodhpur, invited by the Maharaja. The duchess came to visit the Veerni Institute, where she was welcomed with enthusiasm and gratitude by our boarders. The programme of festivities included a welcome song and a *gumar* – the traditional dance that makes brightly coloured costumes twirl. Afterwards our prestigious guest attended a number of classes – IT, English, economics, sewing – and then followed with us all the twists and turns of a match of *kabbadi*, the Indian team sport. After chatting with some of the girls she was very impressed both by our action and by the courageous tenacity of the students. We explained to her that our mission was to provide young women from all castes in the rural Thar Desert region with a good secondary education in a safe and supportive environment. We believe that by giving these women access to education, health and work we can give them the means to become more independent and confident, enabling them to participate responsibly in their community.

The Maharaja supported us for a long time, but we are now completely independent. He and I have remained on good terms. On one of my recent visits with great honour I was invited to a polo tournament. Polo! Very important in India, a precious legacy of British colonisation… In front of the crowd, I had to throw the first ball over a high fence, at the Maharaja's request! Guaranteed humiliation if I missed. Fortunately I succeeded.

We worked under the Maharaja's legal authority until 2015. By then we were running a boarding school, and we had set up an Indian NGO, Veerni Sansthan, also known as the Veerni Institute, a pioneering project in the field of 'caste blindness', with the aim of educating girls from all castes. Recently an upper-caste father came to see me to express his dissatisfaction: in our Institute his daughter had befriended a Dalit, one of the lowest and most despised castes. He asked me to break up this relationship.

'We don't recognise caste, and friendship is an important part of our educational method,' I replied.

He left abruptly.

Two weeks later, he was back with two chocolates in his hands.

'But we have a hundred and ten girls!'

'I'm a poor man, that's all I can give… For my daughter and her friend.'

It was a moving moment, a small step towards global change.

Friendship, a new concept introduced by the Institute! In the villages girls rarely have the time to develop friendships. In fact, this theme was the subject of a literary competition to which the Veerni students contributed poems, plays and essays, a way for them to express the discovery of friendship among themselves. Ten years later we decided to organise such a competition again, this time on the theme of a thought by Isabel Allende: 'We only have what we give.'

Over time my relationship with the Veerni girls and the Institute team has become stronger and more meaningful than I could ever express, because it is based on friendship, love, and years of shared goals, discussions about action, debates about what can be done, consensus-building. An exceptional relationship, a gift of life! I believe that the team, which knows and understands the Project and its mission so well, is guiding Veerni well into the future. Everyone's experience and understanding of the goals are essential, so decisions to move forward are made with their advice in mind. Indeed, they understand village life, they understand the girls, but above all they know what is possible and what still needs to be given up. They work in harmony and create a happy atmosphere for the girls, which is incredibly positive for their development!

This warm benevolence impresses me and arouses my admiration. The team's dedication, the girls' eagerness, their ability to show their joy and happiness expresses everything that is exceptional about our project. These girls are so wonderful, so enthusiastic, so eager to learn! Yet their studies are extremely difficult, as the Indian curriculum is very demanding and must be practised in several languages.

The overall approach of the Veerni staff is to look after the girls' wellbeing, but also to make their lives more relaxed at times. On Sundays they watch a Bollywood film and dance if they feel like it. Once a year, they go on an excursion.

I think the first thing to do is to stay attentive, to be sensitive to the girls' development, to listen to their hopes for the future… Aren't they the hope of the future? They have the same dreams as Western girls, and if Veerni can help them realise their dreams through education they will be stronger and better equipped for the life ahead. We can't take this for granted, because the battle is much harder for them than it is for Western girls. We must not judge entirely by the standards we know, but accept to some extent the culture in which these girls live. Yet on the whole, with the right tools, they will be able to improve their lives, and in time change their society for the better.

All these young ladies are supervised by a senior director, Saroj, and her assistants. When I asked Saroj how she maintained discipline among the one hundred and twelve girls, her answer was clear:

'No smile!'

Saroj is kind, but strict.

A major IT training project was established in 2017 thanks to a generous donor. In 2020 that same donor offered us an additional programme. Tablets and distance learning courses enabled our students to continue their studies, even during the Covid confinement. The result: a 100 per cent exam pass rate!

Another challenge for the Veerni villages, apart from the loss of income exacerbating poverty, is the lack of healthcare leading to untreated illnesses and food shortages. In addition, the return in large numbers of daily-wage workers from India's major cities who have lost their jobs is a cause for concern. This all-male migrant population creates additional problems not only for the spread of disease but also for the safety of vulnerable young girls in the villages. According to the National Crime Record Bureau,

Rajasthan holds the sad record for the highest number of rapes in the entire subcontinent. And the feudal mentality of desert villages, where women are sometimes treated as objects, makes the situation even worse.

Safety at the Institute is a major concern for us. Life in India is not always safe for young women, and a single incident could damage the whole Project. Veerni therefore has a security guard on site all night, and cameras cover the entire premises. Such security is likely to reassure parents. In many respects the girls' school is the safest place, often safer than their villages where houses are open and latrines are not always available for women and girls.

The risk for women and adolescent girls in the villages was notably the lack of latrines, a cause of rape. Women and girls, who cannot be seen, have to go before dawn to relieve themselves outside the village, with all the dangers that these discreet movements represent.

Such crimes often go unpunished, and it's the women who suffer the consequences, which can lead to rejection by their communities, or even suicide.

Teaching young women their rights, how to defend themselves in any environment through education, through building their physical strength, through ensuring their health, will give them the tools to defend themselves when needed. Shobha Choudhary, a former Veerni graduate and child bride who escaped an abusive marriage, is now a number two inspector in the police station in Jaipur. Shobha has demonstrated how women can defend themselves and be a role model for Veerni girls and other women as well.

By educating these young women in a safe environment they will finish their studies, join the work force, and importantly know their human rights. Veerni – the hero woman – makes them strong, assists them in standing up for themselves, to face a better future. The young women will take their rightful place in their families and their communities, contribute fully to situations where decisions concerning all are taken; in a word, be participants in the life of their country. All of Indian society will benefit.

VI
Responding to Covid

Now we face a generational catastrophe
that could waste untold human potential,
undermine decades of progress,
and exacerbate entrenched inequalities.
Antonio Guterres, UN Secretary-General

I n a few sober sentences Mahendra Sharma, Director of the Veerni Institute, summed up the painful period of the Covid pandemic:

It was hard, very hard. It's very hard to imagine the kind of situation we were in. I personally saw piles of bodies piled up in hospitals and so many people died in front of me... pure suffering. We've seen it all, and while it hasn't affected us physically, the tragedy has had a huge emotional impact. We're not the same people we were before Covid, and the ordeals our daughters went through were extremely difficult. There was also a lot of violence and endless problems that the girls had to face in the villages. Some of the girls came back weakened, but one thing never gave way: the support of the villagers, especially the fathers. They believed in us throughout the pandemic! Similarly, the Institute's staff never failed us. Despite the risks, we were constantly supported.

All those who run the Veerni Project in India have been able to look to the future despite the difficulties of the moment. They have shown impressive resilience, demonstrating the incredible team built up around the Project that enables us to look forward. The nature of absolute poverty is difficult to understand in the West. In India we are faced with the poorest of the poor, and the question is how to protect their daughters in the future, their hope for the future. It's fascinating that these terrible times have given rise to a generation of parents who are more inclined to educate. We have learned a lot about how we can reach more girls through technology, and Covid taught us that technology can be used in a different and constructive way.

My last visit to India before the pandemic was in February 2020. We didn't know then that a terrible hurricane was about to hit the world. Complete isolation, no communication, no travel…

A few weeks before the health crisis, we had been planning to take the Veerni Project forward. Indeed, we had just received the indispensable certification for NGOs operating in India. We had fought for five years to obtain these official documents, and were now able to work on various plans.

Then, suddenly, we heard of a pandemic coming from China, and many countries closed their doors. On 21 March we received a call from the Indian authorities ordering us to close our Institute within five hours! We had five hours to send the girls home, and we managed to do it safely. We rented vehicles, contacted some parents, distributed study materials to a few girls, and the process went smoothly, quite harmoniously, despite the panic that gripped us all. Of course, like everywhere else in the world the Covid pandemic turned people's lives upside down. Village life and that of the Veerni Institute were no exception, with adverse effects on health, economies, livelihoods and education.

India was the country hardest hit by the coronavirus. According to Basharat Peer in the *New York Times*, 'The lockdown struck India's poor like a hammer.' Rural areas such as the Thar Desert were severely affected. The Indian government spends just 1 per cent of GDP on healthcare, one of the lowest in the world: this means one hospital bed for over 1,800 Indians and one doctor for over 11,000 patients.

At first, we had no idea how we were going to proceed. Then we started getting calls from parents worried about their daughters staying at home as exams approached, but the education authorities announced that the general exam would be postponed for all students. We therefore continued to make materials available to the girls, their education obviously remaining our primary concern. We then set up a team through which we had many telephone discussions, notably on how to provide study materials to girls in the villages.

As there were no exams yet, we formed a committee with the school administration, who agreed to deliver study materials to us. The challenge was how to get them to 110 girls back in the Institute from 64 different villages, all in the middle of a confinement! Finally, in the last week of April we obtained government authorisation to deliver our educational materials to the villages. A social worker and a driver went from village to village to make the distribution.

By May and June corpses were piling up everywhere, but we were still able to help some families in need, notably by taking the sick to medical facilities.

The school management, for its part, set up WhatsApp groups so that the girls could be reached easily, and the idea then arose to digitise the teaching material and save it on a USB stick to make it available to all. In the second phase of the pandemic our team decided that it would be better to distribute tablets. The computer education programme we launched two years earlier was bearing fruit. If our girls hadn't been trained in computers, nothing would have been possible.

Why tablets? Because in this case no Internet connection

is necessary. I contacted a friend of mine who was working in Delhi at the time to collect these essential tablets. With great difficulty we found the ninety tablets we needed and delivered them to the girls with all the educational content they required. Now all they had to do was switch on the tablet and they could study at home! We also set up a helpline so that if they had any problems they could ask for help.

Of course, we stopped sending our girls to school, and for them we had to transform all the classes at the Institute from 6th to 12th grade. We converted the dormitories into classrooms designated as 'ICT rooms' (Information and Communication Technology). With furniture and giant screens connected to a computer, classes were held at the Institute, with teachers coming in to teach students remotely. An entire school year was spent on this model. The results we achieved were incredible: 100 per cent pass rate!

Normally, once the annual exams are over, the summer vacation lasts a month. This time things were different: girls and parents came to us to tell us that our boarders didn't want to go home: they had to catch up on classes that had been cut during the pandemic. In short, we were asked to organise remedial courses in English, Hindi, mathematics, etc., during the month of August. So we opened a summer school programme in which we not only gave remedial courses but also computer and art lessons, which involved some fifty students – a historic decision for us!

I'd say that technology has been our lifeline. Without it we wouldn't be where we are today. It's as simple as that. The Veerni Institute wouldn't have survived without technology! We wouldn't be able to maintain our programme without technology.

Now, with technology and the computers that help girls succeed so well, we're looking to the creation of a Veerni Hostel housing up to 150 boarders. Perhaps at the same time we could try outreach work with all the girls in the neighbouring villages.

Doesn't technology enable us to teach many pupils from afar?

In terms of hygiene and survival the villagers were going through difficult times, without food and basic necessities. A kit was distributed to each girl with disinfectants, masks, body lotions and sanitary towels, while the villagers could obtain a food kit in such difficult times.

And Covid was still spreading. We feared that some parents would end up withdrawing their daughters from the Veerni programme. Indeed, we received many calls from parents warning us that if the students couldn't return to the Institute they would be sent to their in-laws. About one in two girls had been married off as a child! It was often difficult to feed this extra mouth back home. What's more, a large number of marriages were celebrated during this period, yet another way of easing the financial burden on the girls' parents. We feared that so many lives would be destroyed and futures shattered, as girls married in haste would not always be able to join the Institute later on. However, I have to say that the parents – and especially the fathers – were supportive overall, despite pressure from their community and elders who stubbornly claimed that young girls had no need of education, let alone a trade…

Another Indian tragedy linked to the pandemic was the great migrations that took place. Many men saw their jobs suspended during the period of confinement. What did they do then? They left the big cities – Mumbai, Delhi and many others – to return to the villages they had left to work. Girls called us to report the abuse they were suffering at the hands of these idle men. Our helpline saved more than one girl's life.

In October 2020 the news finally came through: we could reopen the Institute. But with a few restrictions: we were only allowed to take in around thirty girls, and it was hard to choose because all our boarders wanted to come back! We decided to give priority to the oldest girls, who were the most vulnerable in terms of security in the villages. Fortunately, a more flexible approach enabled us to welcome more students.

Alas, at the beginning of 2021 we were hit by the second and deadliest wave, and had to send all the girls home again. Back to where we started. But this time we were prepared! The girls left with educational materials, medical kits and food.

The American journalist Nurith Aizenman, correspondent for National Public Radio, has been following our actions, meeting our pupils, telling stories, writing, and her eye is teaching us to see. After the lockdown she interviewed Komal Rana, a young student in 10th grade. Rana remembers the anxiety that night in the dormitory, as she rushed to pack her things in a hurry.

'Everything was so confusing, everything was closed. I was worried about my family; I was worried about my studies.'

Soon the young girl arrived home, in the village of Jhalamand.

'Everyone in my family started telling my parents that my studies were enough! "What's the point of studying more? It's time to marry her off", they said.'

The confinement turned everything upside down: suddenly school was suspended indefinitely. Rana's parents, who work as day labourers in the construction industry, immediately put her in charge of the household chores expected of a girl in her community.

'We have cattle, I have to look after them,' she says. 'There are all kinds of household chores I have to do. I didn't get a chance to touch my books!'

Yet Rana wanted to become a doctor.

'I was struck by the fact that there wasn't a single doctor in my village,' she explains.

Nevertheless, the pressure to marry off the young girl was becoming even more intense due to another consequence of the pandemic: Covid was making weddings cheap. In normal times families would be happy to host crowds of guests.

Director Mahendra was relieved when the students were able to return.

'I can proudly say that not a single girl was married during the lockdown,' he affirmed.

Yet there were signs that some of the girls had endured a difficult confinement. Eight of them, in particular, seemed terribly withdrawn – students who before the confinement were doing extremely well in their studies. Now they were unwell, had no appetite, weren't taking part in activities… and yet they didn't want to go home, didn't want to meet their parents.

On the strength of his experience, Mahendra realised that these girls might have been victims of sexual violence during the months of confinement in their village. He immediately arranged for a psychologist to visit, but by April 2021 another confinement sent the students home a second time. New pressure to marry Rana off! She avoided the worst by giving private lessons to children in her village, a way of financially helping her family whose father lost his job during the pandemic.

Recently Rana was introduced to a new suitor. The family was enthusiastic and insisted that she finally agree to get married. But this time the father said no! He made a final decision: he would let Rana study at Veerni for as long as she wanted. A happy ending, don't you think?

The pandemic was obviously a difficult time, but we managed to hang in there. Restrictions continued, more or less strictly depending on the period, and we had to close at certain times and reopen with few boarders… an intermittent mode of operation. After that, we had to go through the medical process. We ran a vaccination programme, and all the girls were vaccinated.

For the new academic year 2023 we made major investments in the ITC programme. What was attempted during Covid has become permanent for certain classes. A lot of interesting things happened during that period, transforming destinies. In particular, the girls and their parents wanted to switch to the English language as a medium of education, as they were studying English during the summer. We discussed this, but were faced with a few problems: not all the girls had yet reached the level required to be educated in English. However, we accepted the change for our youngest boarders, who now study in English.

Our constant commitment was never to give up, and always to think about getting back to work as soon as possible. We knew we must never let the Veerni Project die out, because once everything had stopped it would have been extremely difficult to get everything up and running again and get the girls back together. And I saw some Indian associations collapse during this period. But in June 2021, when we finally reopened with full capacity, not a single girl was missing, not one had dropped out of training during the two waves of the Covid. And we're very proud of that!

After Covid we started remedial classes from 5th to 6th grade for girls aged twelve or thirteen, which wasn't part of our original plan: we've always worked for secondary education. But in the villages, so many little girls told us that their father or mother had died because of Covid and that there was no one left to look after them. So we accepted 5th and 6th graders. It wasn't planned. We did it simply because we responded to demand.

While Covid is still active, with its deleterious effects on health and education worldwide, the repercussions on young girls are numerous in some countries. The rate of child marriages in India has soared since the start of the pandemic, as desperate families see no other solution. New bills, such as the one currently under discussion in Uttar Pradesh which proposes to limit the number of children to two, will further skew the figures in favour of boys.

In many cases, it is young people who have suffered most from the pandemic. In the developing world, the loss of education for girls is dramatic, and years of progress could be wiped out in a short space of time: all the advances made for girls worldwide are under threat. Worldwide, 1.6 billion children have been affected by the pandemic, and some girls may never return to school. They are now particularly vulnerable, as schools are often the only places where they are safe.

The long-term mission of the Veerni Project remains the education of girls, but our most important role now is also to protect them. The safety of our boarders is a priority. Veerni operates like a family and has always been led by the heart, a relationship of trust built up through thirty years of presence and initiative in the villages.

VII
Portraits of Daily Life

It's about discovering who you really are,
letting yourself be who you are...

Thuksey Rinpoche
(quoted by Andrew Harvey in *A Journey in Ladakh*)

Protecting our young girls and leading them towards
education sometimes means enlisting the help of local
Rajasthani personalities from all castes: lawyers, university
professors and even judges at the High Court in Jodhpur. Indeed,
we have sometimes needed this jurisdiction to try and free child
brides from their bonds.

For example, Shobha told the High Court how she had been
forced into marriage at the age of eight. A naive little girl, she
had happily accepted her fate.

'I had beautiful new clothes,' she said. 'I didn't know the
meaning of marriage. I was happy.'

Basically, at the time, nothing changed for her. So, what if
she had a husband? Generally, in her village, when the bride is
too young, she doesn't immediately settle down with her new
husband. She stays with her parents until her fifteenth birthday,
and only then is she sent to her in-laws. What happens then?
The husband's mother assigns her daughter-in-law whatever
tasks she sees fit... and the bride has to follow orders without
question or complaint!

Shobha was born in Rajwa, a village some thirty kilometres
from Jodhpur, a place of extreme poverty where most women

are illiterate, where girls are married off before the age of ten, and where many girls have had their dreams snuffed out and been sent to their in-laws before they've even had a chance to live outside the four walls of the house. At a very early age these girls are burdened with domestic responsibilities, and sometimes even experience early motherhood, often with disastrous consequences for their health.

Veerni stepped in: we opened a sewing and literacy centre in Rajwa, as well as health information sessions. Shobha had been one of the pupils at the literacy centre: her exceptional qualities were quickly spotted and she joined the Veerni Institute to begin a real education. Indeed, she followed the classes with passion and intelligence, her self-confidence grew, she finally refused to return to the village and even more so to join her husband. She was already thinking about how to get a divorce! But the family pressure and threats were so heavy that she had to resolve to return to the village. And if she didn't? The shame would have fallen on her father, her mother, her siblings, her cousins... Indeed, according to ancestral customs, her own relatives could be expelled from the village for not respecting the contract made with the groom. The village elders forced Shobha's parents to send her to her in-laws' house in the village of Keru. She spent a total of four days with her husband, was raped, and eventually fled.

'My husband and his family took me in harshly, didn't allow me to work and treated me like an animal,' she recounts.

She then went to the police station, but the officers on duty wouldn't listen, and, at the same time the whole village turned against her: she had dared to flee her in-laws and leave Keru! But Shobha remained steadfast and sought the help of government authorities to have her marriage, illegal under Indian law, annulled. This emblematic struggle was followed by the town's newspapers and local TV stations, her story was publicised, the young girl was applauded by some… and received death threats from others.

Finally, after a long struggle, she got what she wanted: the High Court of Jodhpur granted her a divorce. Cynthia Gurney, a journalist with *National Geographic*, was moved by her story and made a donation to finance Shobha's university studies. She studied, joined the police, and was recently appointed commissioner. Her professional goal: to specialise in enforcing the law banning child marriage. 'Before my very eyes, I will never again allow child marriages to occur. I will save every girl,' she said.

Sunita, also from a village in Rajasthan, joined the Veerni Institute to prepare for university studies. With us, she successfully completed her studies in English, Economics, Sociology and Political Science. Brilliant and athletic, she represented her school in field hockey and long jump at championships, took a computer course and learned all about accounting software. Sunita blossomed and soon her leadership qualities became evident to all. She continued her empowerment process and soon realised that, as a woman, she could become both socially and financially independent. At the invitation of the International Women's Health Coalition, Sunita, then a third-year student, travelled to New York to speak at the annual gala dinner. Following the first speaker, Mayor Michael Bloomberg, Sunita captivated the audience with her impassioned speech on how education had transformed her life: she received a standing ovation from the four hundred and fifty guests.

Back in Jodhpur, Sunita completed a postgraduate diploma in Arts and a master's degree in Economics and Social Work. In 2014, she met Marion Richardson, an Israeli volunteer who had come to Veerni to share her expertise in business management. On some days Marion would eat meals at the Institute with the girls, help them improve their English conversation skills, and organise craft activities. Together with Vimlesh, our nurse,

Marion took part in an educational programme on hygiene and cleanliness, while accompanying Mahendra, our Director, on outings to the surrounding villages.

When Marion first met Sunita, she was twenty-six years old and working as an enrolment assistant for a local girls' college in the city of Jodhpur. That was the start of a wonderful friendship. In the hours and days, they spent together, Marion encouraged Sunita to express herself for herself, to read English literature, to watch films, not to be afraid of the matrimonial pressures exerted by her family. In return, Sunita taught Marion the rudiments of Indian cooking. All in all, the Israeli became the young Indian's godmother, supporting her through good times and bad.

And there were some difficult days. Sunita was always caught between the traditional village lifestyle and the more independent city lifestyle. She still often visits her parents in the village, but dreams of a career in the Indian administration. This is probably her greatest challenge today. For the time being, with a few friends Sunita has set up a small classroom in the city where she and her colleagues are trying to teach the basics of reading, writing and arithmetic to street kids who live by the side of highways and have no access to education.

As a result, Sunita is very much involved in volunteering and giving, so she is trying to create a local group of volunteers ready to help poor children, educate them and fight their addiction to dangerous substances. Sunita has been lucky enough to receive, and generously she wants to give back what she has been offered. So many people take but never give! As a graduate of Veerni, she knows she is now capable of passing on what she has learned. A fine example of how Veerni can profoundly transform the surrounding society.

In rural India, most fathers want only one thing for their daughters: a husband capable of providing for them. Lumbaram, on the other hand, wanted something different for his daughter

Durga: luck! And yet, despite her father's belief that marriage was a mistake for his daughter, Durga was promised to a man. On her wedding day Durga cried when the village women put on her wedding dress, a red sari with golden ornaments; she cried when she saw her husband; she cried as she walked with him around the ritual fire… She cried because she didn't want to get married. Even Lumbaram wanted to cry, but he wasn't allowed to.

On her wedding day Durga was fifteen years old, her husband almost twice that. Lumbaram had agreed to the union because the families had put pressure on him. Marrying Durga would give the father's younger brother a wife from that family, with no extra cost to either side! She was exchanged for a wife for her uncle, to a man who was twenty-five years older than her and had a drinking problem. A terrifying exchange, but quite common in rural India, where there are too many men for too few women. Why this disproportion? Because, for decades, unborn girls have been aborted or killed at birth.

But what happened after Durga's wedding is exceptional. Lumbaram took his daughter aside, looked at her with tear-filled eyes, and promised he'd make it up to her. He didn't give up, he fought, and eight years after the marriage he finally obtained a divorce for his daughter!

Lumbaram and his family live in Meghwalon Ki Dhani, a forgotten village of six hundred and fifty people, a village of nowhere connected to nothing, not a single road to get there, just a sandy track and a path lined with shrubs along which wild peacocks peck. A forgotten village because it's a village of Dalits, the 'untouchables'. Lumbaram's house is a little way from the village, a one-storey building with a fireplace in the courtyard.

Today, Lumbaram serves as a construction worker in Jodhpur, but he recounts how, as a child, he didn't eat every day: his family was so poor. And yet he walked seven kilometres to school every day, and was lucky enough to attend classes for years, until the 5th grade. Despite this schooling, he could neither read nor write. So, he first became a farmer, like his father, and later a labourer like all the men in the village. But Lumbaram is different from the others: he doesn't drink alcohol, he practises yoga, and above all – an astonishing originality – he rejoiced at the birth of each of his three daughters.

As we have seen, sons are typically valued as the parents' old-age stick: they work, they bring money… Very often daughters eat less than their brothers at the family table, and have to work harder. Fortunately, things were different for Durga. A secret pact had even been demanded by her father for the marriage: the girl would stay with her parents until she was fifteen, and until then she would go to school. Lumbaram wanted his child to get what he had been denied: an education and a good job. When she was a child her father took her to elementary school every day – the only girl in the village to go to class! A few years later, at the age of thirteen, Durga was admitted to the Veerni Institute. The other fathers in the village were outraged: how could anyone send their daughter alone to a foreign city?

Durga, a hard-working student, was the first 'untouchable' to take part in the programme; she was open, warm… but after a brief return to her family she became silent and withdrawn. She told us she would commit suicide if she were sent back to that man, her husband.

To support the father, the boarding school agreed to take in his three daughters, to relieve him of the cost of education. When Durga graduated five years later, Veerni offered to finance her university education, but the husband became irritated. He turned to the village council of elders and demanded that the marriage be enforced. The elders said they respected Lumbaram's love for his daughter, but how could the husband accept a union without his wife? The council proposed a barter: Durga's marriage could be annulled in return for 'severance pay' of 450,000 rupees (almost 6,000 euros). A gigantic sum, unimaginable for Lumbaram.

But Durga continued her studies, taking courses in politics, history and sociology, and was the first in her village to attend university.

So Lumbaram didn't send his daughter back to her husband. As punishment he was excluded from his community, his neighbours no longer spoke to him, he was no longer allowed to use the village's main street... But he would have done anything for his daughters!

The Veerni Institute then helped him hire a lawyer and file a complaint: if the marriage was officially declared illegal, the husband could not demand a financial settlement. The court ruled in Lumbaram's favour, but in the eyes of the elders the marriage was still valid. The judge therefore referred the case to a counselling centre, which asked Durga how she felt about her husband, what her future plans were and whether her husband had prevented her from achieving them. The husband had to show up, too. The appointments were a burden for him: he had to keep going to town and answering questions about a woman who didn't live with him. He begged the judges to let him go. Indeed, his marriage to Durga had become so burdensome that he finally asked the officials to dissolve it. In exchange, he would relinquish his claims against Lumbaram.

After the divorce the father once again became a full member of the village community. Durga finished university and married a man her own age who works in the police force.

We could go on, telling other adventures, other crazy stories, other dramatic twists and turns... Every girl who comes to Veerni to emancipate herself and change her destiny has to fight against traditions and prejudices.

Guddi arrived at the Veerni Institute in 2008, at the age of fourteen. A member of the Bishnoi community in the village of Unchiarda, she had been promised in marriage at the age of four to a man fifteen years her senior. Her family lived in an isolated house in the desert, some distance from the village. The Bishnois are traditionally opium dealers, and their caste is criminal and violent: her mother had lost an eye in a fight. Although the family owned a buffalo, most of their income came from smuggling. Her sister, who is illiterate, returned to her parents' home with two children, since her husband was in trouble with the law. Guddi asked me to meet her father to explain the Veerni Project, and he finally agreed to let her continue her studies on condition that she could find a good job and earn money in the future, as he would never force her to join her husband.

We were concerned for Guddi, since her family situation was a constant source of worry and we feared she was on the verge of anorexia. She was monitored and counselled by Dr Bhansali, our psychologist, and regained her spirits and the will to move forward.

From the point of view of the Institute, Guddi's admission was a great feat. There was opposition to the admission of girls from lower castes, since most of the girls still belonged to higher castes. We had pledged to respect caste diversity, and Guddi was a brilliant student, so there was no reason why she shouldn't be accepted. Unfortunately, from the outset she was discriminated against, not least by the school principal. What's more, the management made fun of her father, who regularly visited her wearing a *dhoti*, the traditional dress of village men. Guddi turned out to be a brilliant student, lost some of the roughness of her background and blended in with the other students. She graduated in 2010 and went on to university, where, still supported by Veerni, she obtained a bachelor of arts degree. At the hotel in a wing of the Maharaja's luxury palace in Jodhpur she was the first non-Rajput apprentice – i.e.

not from a high caste. But prejudices die hard: when I visited her, she was in charge of the ladies' room, a job reserved for women of low status.

At Guddi's wedding in her village at the age of twenty-one, Brigadier Shakti Singh, Director of the Maharaja's Trust and the Veerni Project, was present, accompanied by Her Highness the Maharani of Jodhpur, the Maharaja's wife. Brigadier Singh gave a speech and encouraged the young bride to have only two children. It was unusual, to say the least, for a young woman like Guddi, from a despised caste, to have such prestigious guests at her wedding.

After working at the hotel for a few months Guddi decided to leave her apprenticeship and join her husband. She came with him to the Veerni office to tell us of her decision. I regret that decision, since I am convinced that she could have made a fine career in the hotel business, but we obviously respected her choice.

More recently, at the end of 2022, I visited Guddi in her village. She is now a government health worker, has two daughters and a son, owns a scooter, and goes out to work in the villages. As for her husband, he is a farmer and seems a good man, and the family will soon be moving into a new, bigger and better house. In a way Guddi's story is one of success: doesn't she come from a community where it's very difficult to get even the slightest education and training? Now a mother, she is educating her daughters, has high ambitions for them, and plans to send them to the Veerni Institute in the future, so that they will be perfectly educated. Guddi has changed the future. Today she's an independent young woman, happily married.

VIII
Should we Conclude?

The sky is filled with stars, invisible by day.
Henry Wadsworth Longfellow

All we really possess is what we can give, however modestly. A spiritually successful life involves kindness and caring. What if it consisted of having worked to leave the world a little better place than we found it? My wish is to see the Veerni Project continue to do what it does best, which is to educate girls and raise them to a level of excellence.

With that in mind I think I've played my part, and I'm now thinking about the succession. It has to be established before the moment comes, I know, and that's why I've brought younger women into the Veerni Project, who are now the same age as I was in 1993, when I launched this wonderful adventure. You have to accept that a different generation can do things differently. My role has been to develop the Project, to guide it for many years. Now it's time for others to take it over, to maintain its spirit, to make it develop, to maintain its being and its heart.

I believe that a successful life can consist in leaving the world in a slightly better state than we found it. A small contribution to the happiness of all.

Is this a form of conclusion? Does one really have to draw a life's commitment to a conclusion? I don't know what form my commitment will take in the years to come, but I do know that, in one way or another, I will continue to fight for women throughout the world and for the young girls of Rajasthan in particular.

Recent times have presented Veerni with many challenges, the greatest of any in its three-decade-long history. Social tensions, community confrontations and pandemics have shaken up lives and altered plans. The staff have been nothing short of heroic in their devotion to the girls and their families, unfailingly helping our boarders to gain access to education, to stay in school, and to keep alive the hope of a better future. Our long-term relationship with the villages has made all this possible; Veerni has earned the trust of the villagers for three decades.

Why is the work of the Veerni Project still so important? Why has it never been so crucial? Despite the progress that has been made, India remains a country where there is still an enormous amount to be done on behalf of women. In its own way the Veerni Project is helping to bring about this much-needed and much-awaited change. Veerni is infinitely small, no doubt, lost in the Indian tide, perhaps, but its significance goes far beyond its achievements, I'm convinced. For our daughters, a bright future is always a promise kept. Could Veerni become an example, a model?

We are making progress and achieving significant successes. For example, in the recent past not one of the thirty-five married girls at our Institute was sent home to her husband by her family. Not one! Remarkably, fathers are now very supportive of their daughters' education. Previously only mothers encouraged them to study. This transformation of male attitudes is largely due to the involvement of the whole family in the development of the Veerni girls. Everyone has realised that education is a sound investment for the future.

And yet, in a world that is changing so fast, with international relations becoming more complicated by the day, the future seems more unfathomable than ever. On every level the planet is hiccupping: climate, economy, epidemics… Where are we heading? Democracy itself seems to be called into question. Yet it is so important to defend it. Although imperfect, it is the only system that allows human development to take place in freedom and without fear, a system that allows us to live together in peace…

In this new world that is taking shape, women's wellbeing – in all its aspects – is essential to human development. The participation of women in the life of their communities and in the destiny of their country is indispensable and eagerly awaited.

All those involved with me in the Veerni Project are doing their part to move towards this future, to make some progress towards a better world. Even if, as I said, our action is just a drop in the ocean.

IX

Hope – Once you Choose
Hope All is Possible

Life is like a bicycle.
You have to move forward
so as not to lose your balance.
Albert Einstein

Veerni survived Covid – never gave up hope, kept moving forward and came out stronger. The need for girls' education has never been greater, and Veerni can contribute to this key development and make sure young Indian women have their rightful place in Indian society.

We cannot fully comprehend in the West what the Veerni team experienced during Covid. The full extent of the lockdown, the lines in front of the hospitals, deaths omnipresent in the town and in the villages. Members of the families of the team experienced losses and illness.

As India is recognised as a land of diversity, so the impact of Covid-19 was diverse and countless. The most notable effects of lockdown included disturbances in children's education and devastated occupations resulting in parents' loss of income, creating more poverty. Given the unavailability of jobs and income in the cities, many migrant workers went home. Some died on the roads to their villages after trains were cancelled. Some of those who got home, idle, at times made life risky in village settings for the girls. Village houses are usually left unlocked, and girls sent out to fetch water were not safe from the bad intentions of idle men. Additionally, the disease and fear of it affected people's health and their quality of life.

However, importantly, India is a resilient country. It arranged vaccination for its population – an incredible achievement – and life is now back to what is was prior to the pandemic in terms of employment.

The Veerni Project never stood still, always kept going, kept the faith of the villagers alive. The Project is heading for new experiences, new ventures, and gaining strength. The girls are all back and more robust than ever in their dedication to their studies.

Plans for the future include a new permanent home which will soon be a reality; giving scope to conduct community programmes, much in demand from the villagers, particularly remedial education for village girls who dropped out of education during Covid; to run training centres; to widen the scope of careers for the young women who graduate.

Veerni's reach in the community can expand and help more young women.

Veerni never stands still and looks to the future so that many more young women have the chance to fulfill their dreams.

Veerni is a project with a heart, faith in the future and the resolve to make it happen.

I would like to end with a favorite quotation from Teilhard de Chardin that tells the story of Veerni:

To give oneself. To leave the world a little better, whether by a healthy child, a garden patch or a redeemed social condition; to have played and laughed with enthusiasm and sung with exultation; to know even one life has breathed easier because you have lived, this is to have succeeded.

COVID PANDEMIC

Mahendra Sharma, Director of the Veerni Institute

During the time of Covid I stood on the edge of a great responsibility. The Veerni Project, which meant so much to Veerni girls, hung in the balance. Isolation surrounded me, casting me into a sea of uncertainty. The lockdown felt like a storm tearing at the heart of Veerni. Phone calls became my lifeline, keeping me connected with the Veerni team. News of abuse against girls trapped in their homes echoed down the line. Parents, worried about their daughters' futures, sought answers from us. Community pressures mounted – whispers of child marriages and girls being sent to in-laws hung heavy in the air.

The girls themselves called me, their voices laced with fear. Basic necessities like sanitary napkins were scarce, and the thought of marriage loomed like a dark cloud. There were moments when the lockdown felt like a death knell for Veerni, a project I held so dear.

But amidst the despair, a flicker of hope ignited. Through countless phone calls with Ms Jacqueline we formulated a plan, a lifeline for Veerni. Our mission was twofold:

- **Education Uninterrupted:** 'School at the Doorstep' and 'Digital Education' were born. Our team, braving the lockdown with limited permits, ventured out to villages, delivering learning materials and tablets. This ensured that the girls stayed connected to their studies despite the isolation.
- **Health and Support:** 'Health Outreach' programmes gave villagers vital information to stay safe from the

virus. Additionally, we distributed food and hygiene kits to Veerni girls and families in need.

Every step was an uphill battle. Lockdown restrictions were strict, the streets patrolled by watchful eyes. Fear of police brutality hung in the air. But fuelled by an unwavering commitment to Veerni we persisted.

With the help of a supportive school administration, digital educational content was created. Tablets, procured from Delhi, became gateways to learning, delivered by our dedicated team despite the challenges. Food and hygiene kits provided a much-needed safety net for vulnerable families.

After the lockdown, when we reopened the Veerni Institute, we introduced an ICT – Information and Communications Technology – programme. The academic year saw substantial investments in upgrading the Institute's technology infrastructure. On the ground floor a remarkable transformation occurred: there was state-of-the-art equipment and technology surpassing what local schools could offer. This not only enriched the learning experience but also provided a much-needed convenience for the Veerni girls. Their education thrived in the secure environment of the Institute, guided by dedicated teachers in four well-equipped ICT classrooms.

Parents supported Veerni and promised they would continue Veerni's efforts to keep their daughters engaged with education. In these very difficult times the parents kept their faith in the project, building on the established trust over many years.

Despite these immense challenges, all the Veerni girls achieved a phenomenal 100 per cent result! This accomplishment is a powerful testament to the dedication of both the girls and the Veerni team. In the face of adversity, they not only persevered, they excelled.

MY OWN COVID STORY

The lockdown in Jodhpur was a scene ripped from a nightmare. As one of the few with government permission to venture out, I witnessed a desolate landscape – piles of unclaimed bodies, a chilling reminder of the pandemic's brutality.

Meanwhile, Covid had infiltrated my own family. My brother, hospitalised for twenty-five harrowing days, battled the virus relentlessly. His condition remained precarious, and for those weeks contact was limited to terse updates from doctors. He survived, but his physical strength remains compromised.

Tragedy struck again. My once-healthy uncle fell victim to the virus, spending twelve days in the hospital before succumbing. Finding a bed had been a desperate fight, and the inability to hold a proper funeral amplified our heartache.

Amidst this personal turmoil, a friend called for help. Her husband had contracted Covid. Leveraging my access, I secured a hospital bed, and thankfully he recovered. But the respite was short-lived. His mother soon fell ill, and despite my frantic efforts a bed couldn't be found. After a gruelling seven hours she lost her battle in front of my eyes.

Everywhere I turned hospitals overflowed, and despair hung heavy in the air. I was exposed too much. These horrific sights and experiences left a deep emotional scar.

Despite the personal devastation – losing my uncle and my friend's mother, witnessing my loved ones' struggle, and being haunted by the piles of the deceased – Veerni thrived. While countless organisations crumbled, we persevered. This success stands as a testament to the unwavering spirit of the Veerni team and a ray of hope in those dark times.

Covid may have scarred me profoundly, but it also solidified Veerni's resilience. We emerged stronger, forever marked by the struggle, but determined to continue our mission.

THREE VEERNI GIRLS:
SHOBHA, DURGA AND SUNITA

Shobha Choudary

Shobha Choudary, a young woman from Rajwa village, Rajasthan, fought for her education and freedom from child marriage. Married at eight, she found hope at the Veerni Institute, a boarding school for girls. After completing high school, Shobha dreamt of a life beyond societal constraints.

The Veerni Project's support empowered her. She pursued higher education, a computer application diploma, and a hotel management course. Despite family pressure to rejoin her husband, Shobha bravely refused. With Veerni's backing, she filed for annulment, citing the illegality of child marriage. Her story garnered media attention, and finally, the Jodhpur High Court granted her a divorce.

Shobha's journey is one of resilience. Today, a police inspector, she empowers others to fight for their rights. The Veerni Institute, she says, is the reason she can finally claim her independence.

Durga

Durga, a Dalit girl from a village plagued by child marriage, found refuge at the Veerni Institute. When pressure mounted to send her back to her illiterate, much older husband, Veerni intervened. Her father, Lumbha Ram, initially succumbed to societal pressure.

However, a meeting with Veerni officials transformed him. Lumbha Ram realized the injustice he had done to his daughter. He not only supported Durga's education but vowed to end child marriage in his community. This story exemplifies the power of education and the Veerni Project's dedication to social change.

Sunita

Sunita, born into poverty, blossomed at the Veerni Institute. Her leadership qualities shone, and she embraced the path to empowerment. After excelling in her studies, she became a role model for her peers.

Sunita's journey wasn't without challenges. Invited to speak at an international women's event, she impressed audiences with her story of transformation. However, returning to her village, she grappled with the contrast between American and Indian realities.

Marion Richardson, a Veerni volunteer, became a pillar of support. With Marion's encouragement, Sunita overcame her shyness and honed her English skills. This friendship helped Sunita navigate societal pressures regarding marriage.

Today, Sunita stands out. Married later than is customary in India, she chose a partner who matched her educational background. Now, she's actively involved in giving back to her community, striving to educate underprivileged children and fight against substance abuse. Sunita embodies the transformative power of the Veerni Institute and its lasting impact on society.

TESTIMONIALS

Sophie Fauchier

Since I came in 2015, I have been touched by its unique holistic and family approach which goes beyond education. Despite its small scale, it has changed the lives of countless girls in hard-to-reach areas.

I am deeply proud to be part of such an initiative".

Joan Gurry

In 2006, I connected with Veerni through Cathy Callender, embarking on a transformative journey in Jodhpur. Veerni's holistic approach earned trust, paving the way for empowering adolescent girls through education. Returning two years later, I witnessed the profound impact of our work as families embraced sending daughters to school. Guided by Jacqueline's spirit of generosity, Veerni embodies resilience, propelling lives towards boundless promise. I am deeply proud of our collective achievements, knowing each life touched now radiates with purpose..

Marion Richardson

In autumn 2013, I met Jacqueline in New York and heard for the first time about the Veerni Institute. Three months later I was already working side by side with Mahendra in his office, sharing life with the Veerni girls. Over the next 4 months I understood that Veerni is an institute of strong and brave young girls whose futures have been changed by the unswerving vision and continuing determination of Jacqueline de Chollet. It was then too that I met up with Sunita, a graduate of Veerni and an independent and free-thinking young woman. We are still often in contact and I was honoured to have been invited to her wedding in Jodhpur a few years ago. I look forward to my next visit to Jodhpur to see the newly constructed Veerni Institute's building.

Jasmine Schmidt

Volunteering at the Veerni Institute was a life-changing experience. I had the privilege of meeting very kind, passionate and inspiring people dedicated to empowering young women. The time I spent with them opened my eyes to the incredible work they do and reminded me of the profound difference we can make when we come together and support each other. Thank you, dear Veerni family, for all that you do.

Sita Schutt

Looking back, I taught the girls in the villages in 2004 in my month volunteering at Veerni. It taught me the most important lessons about education and development. At the time, the classes were based in villages mostly outdoors and had to contend with the heat and the distance. This was before the Veerni institute existed. I had never seen so little material support for education as in these villages but also never seen so much willingness to learn and try new things. I was so warmly welcomed into their lives. We ended up acting, painting and making a calendar because there was a limit to how much English I could teach them in just one month. The contrast between then and now is enormous.

Mirjam Vanderven

I taught English and arts from June 1 until 5 August 2006. My main goal for the English classes was to improve the communication skills of the girls and to practice speaking out loud, thereby increasing their confidence. There were a total of 58 girls, spread out over classes 5-11.

It was wonderful to see the girls develop, even after just five weeks. There was a distinct difference between the first and the last week, with most girls appearing more self-assured in the end.

I very much enjoyed my time with Veerni. I learned much about the position and challenges of women in Rajasthan. Hopefully I made a small contribution in increasing the English skills and confidence level of the boarding school girls.

ACKNOWLEDGEMENTS

It is sweeter to give than to receive.

Epicurus

Many thanks are due for the long period of thirty years. My first thanks goes to my family, my children Alexandra, Sophie and Michael and their husbands and wife; Peter Fairbairn, Nick Veronis and Fiona Marr, for their support in all of the Veerni endeavours, and to my stepdaughter Emily and her husband Charles Boileau. This support has been important in light of the many challenges that Veerni has faced over the years. Whether visiting, fundraising, being a sounding board, or just listening, the whole family, whether children, in-laws or grandchildren, you have all been there for me and made a meaningful and long-lasting contribution to the Project.

Importantly, I wish to turn to the persons who inspired me: Joan Dunlop and Adrienne Germain, champions of women's health rights in the developing world; to my friend Maja Daruwalla from Delhi who helped me found the Project in 1993 and remained a source of wisdom in navigating at times difficult waters; to the Maharaja of Jodhpur, whose friendship was invaluable to me during many years and whose Trust sheltered Veerni at an important moment in the Project's life; to Her Highness Hemlata Rajye for her commitment to Veerni, hosting the village women's meetings and encouraging the girls in the initial Institute with their studies. Thanks importantly to Brigadier Shakti Singh, who took over the direction of the Veerni Project and led us through the first important years of girls' education; to Dr K.C. Joshi, Veerni's physician, whose wisdom and compassion have been exemplary and who was a hero during the onset of HIV/AIDS which was rampant for some years in the Veerni villages.

My special thanks go also to the members of the Veerni Project's initial foundation in the USA, the Global Foundation for Humanity, created in 1993, that funded the Veerni Project entirely at the beginning and partly for so many years. Members of the GFH board visited Veerni on several occasions and gave the Project crucial moral as well as financial support in difficult times. Some members spent months on site, such as Joan Gurry, and Professor Shirley Johnson-Lans of Vassar College who has published academic research worldwide.

My thanks also to board members: Maryanne Schwalbe, champion of refugee women throughout the world, for her wisdom and generosity of heart; to William McArthur, a long-time Veerni friend, who visited the project, for his advice and great generosity; to Paul Zuckerman, expert on developing countries, especially India, whose advice and support have been invaluable for so many years. To my daughter Sophie, a trustee of the Global Foundation for Humanity for some twenty years, and her husband Nick also a board member, for their support. To Puneet Batra, Garima Maheshwari and Sube Parmar, a recent member of the board, and her husband Ramesh, for their ongoing support. All have visited the Project over the years.

All of them visited Veerni over the years.

My very special thanks and gratefulness go to Kathy Fico, the Administrative Assistant of the Global Foundation, for all the work accomplished and her devotion over the past thirty years. There are few words to express our appreciation of all the time and wisdom she devoted to the Foundation and to the Veerni Project.

My heartfelt thanks go to the outstanding members of the Veerni Foundation, set up in 2017 with the invaluable help of Pierre Henchoz, who has given us the benefit of his international experience, his wisdom, generosity and advice. To Françoise Zweifel, who has devoted herself to the work of the Foundation's administration and whose international experience has been invaluable, as well as many contacts she brought to the Project and identifying donors. To Sophie Fauchier, Sophie Maam as she is known in the project, who has demonstrated her love through her relationship with the people on the ground, her beautiful photographs, her constant efforts to find donors, and her glamorous fundraising weekends in Venice. Thanks also to Patrick Fauchier and the talented Fauchier family. To my son Michael Marr, a vital and dedicated source of sound advice, President of the Fondation Veerni, who lives in Australia; he has visited Veerni on several occasions with groups of people. Importantly, Veerni owes its ICT programme to his link to a major donor; without it the Project would have had little chance of surviving the Covid epidemic. A highly important member is Sita Schutt, a volunteer in 2004, whose sensitivity to the plight of young Indian girls gained on site in her work in the villages, and her academic background, make her an ideal link with Indian reality, together with her help in finding donors and writing reports. Thanks too to her team at Prospero World.

All of the members of the Global Foundation for Humanity and the Fondation Veerni have guided and ensured the longtime existence of the Veerni Project and have helped it to thrive in so many vital ways, including their individual generosity and their relentless work in finding donors on behalf of the Project.

My deepest gratitude goes to all our generous donors over these thirty years, mainly in the UK, Switzerland, the USA, and ASIA PACIFIC. Their support has been vital for the Veerni Project, enabling us to envisage a solid future, to progress and develop in response to changing demands. We owe them all a massive 'thank you' for their commitment over the years and for their unwavering belief in the Project. You know who you are, and we owe you a huge debt of gratitude.

My forever gratitude to Anne Vincent, who accompanied me on my trips to India for many years and was a strong presence in the Veerni villages. Often fearless, as there were at times occasions when village men did not make us feel welcome, she remained undeterred and inspired immediate respect! She was a source of counsel, and through the Association du Projet Veerni raised substantial funds over the years in Switzerland. In 2017 she created the Association du Projet Veera, which finances the university studies of young girls, a number of them from Veerni. She will always be an important part of Veerni.

My gratitude to all the volunteers from different countries, the USA, UK, India, Ireland, Australia and Canada, for the time they have given to the Project, among them my granddaughter Eleanor St Aubyn and Mirjam Vanderven. These volunteers gave their time first in the villages and then at the Institute.

Importantly Joan Gurry who spent several months in the project, had firsthand knowledge of the country and whose wisdom and advice were invaluable. She later joined the board of the Global Foundation for Humanity. Marion Richardson, from Israel, who spent weeks in India and became a second mother to a young woman from Veerni and continues to mentor her. Her support has been key to this young woman's success in life. I would also like to thank our two English volunteers, Christine Kissinger and Wendy Jameson whose contribution in teaching and nursing was invaluable. To Jasmine Schmidt, a recent volunteer who spent weeks at Veerni and was very popular with the girls.

To the many volunteers Veerni who spent time over many years, in teaching and nursing.

I wish to express my thanks to Deeya Sharma, originally from Jodhpur and who lives in Seattle in the US who through her high school and then her college organization, WE CARE, raised funds for Veerni and will work with others on the Veerni archives at Princeton. We are very thankful to have a young group of supporters.

I would to express all my appreciation and thanks to Sheila

Coker Besson, presently the incoming administrator of the Fondation Veerni for her invaluable work on the Veerni Project archives: it took several months to track down and gather and send thirty years of reports, films and photographs for the archives of Princeton University in the USA. Sheila continues the work of updating the archives on a regular basis.

My heartfelt thanks go to the Veerni Project team, who have devoted so many years to the development of the Project and to the wellbeing of the girls through a 'holistic' approach. Together and individually, they have supported and encouraged the girls, looked after their education and their health, and worked to develop their faith in themselves. In short, Veerni helped these young women transform their destinies, realize their dreams, giving them the confidence to take their rightful place in their communities and in Indian society.

My special thanks go to the Director, Mahendra Sharma, for guiding Veerni through so many changes over the years; for his devotion and understanding of the local culture, crucial to the success of the Veerni Project; for establishing Veerni as an independent NGO, a near miracle; and now guiding Veerni to the establishment of a permanent home, the most important undertaking for the future of the project. Special thanks too to Vimlesh Sharma, Project Director and Head Nurse; to Syona Rao, Volunteer Nurse; to Mahinder Singh, Project Administrator; and to all the Project staff, including the girls' guardians, cooks, guards, teachers, e-tutors and sports coaches; and to members of the Veerni board, the Rev. Manish Rao and Mr Pradeep Gandhi among them.

Last but not least, my thanks to the Veerni girls for their courage and perseverance in attending school and passing their exams; to all who contribute to the success of the Veerni Project and help to achieve a 100 per cent pass rate in school exams. This success is due to everyone's dedication.

My thanks to Monsieur Pierre-Marcel Favre and to Editions

Favre and his team for their enthusiasm in publishing the book initially in French. My warm thanks to Emmanuel Haymann for all his hard work and understanding of this long journey through time and space. And above all to Françoise Zweifel, who was the soul behind the publishing of the book and who introduced me to Unicorn. There are few words to express to her my own profound appreciation and gratitude from us all.

My deep appreciation to Lord Strathcarron for the publication by Unicorn of my story, and my thanks to Ryan Gearing and Emily Lane and to all involved in the English version of the book.

Genolier, April 2024